Q, the Earliest Gospel

Q, the Earliest Gospel

An Introduction to the Original Stories and Sayings of Jesus

John S. Kloppenborg

Westminster John Knox Press
LOUISVILLE • LONDON

The appendix was originally published as *The Critical Edition of Q: A Synopsis, Including the Gospels of Matthew and Luke, Mark and Thomas, with English, German and French Translations of Q and Thomas.* Hermeneia Supplements. Leuven: Peeters; Minneapolis: Fortress Press, 2000. Reprinted with minor revisions with the permission of the editors: James M. Robinson, Paul Hoffmann, and John S. Kloppenborg.

Book design by Sharon Adams
Cover design by designpointinc.com

First edition
Published by Westminster John Knox Press
Louisville, Kentucky

This book is printed on acid-free paper that meets the American National Standards Institute Z39.48 standard. ∞

PRINTED IN THE UNITED STATES OF AMERICA

08 09 10 11 12 13 14 15 16 17 — 10 9 8 7 6 5 4 3 2 1

Library of Congress Cataloging-in-Publication Data

Kloppenborg, John S., 1951–
    Q, the earliest Gospel : an introduction to the original stories and sayings of Jesus / John S. Kloppenborg. — 1st ed.
        p. cm.
    Includes bibliographical references (p.   ).
    ISBN 978-0-664-23222-1 (alk. paper)
    1. Q hypothesis (Synoptics criticism)   2. Two source hypothesis (Synoptics criticism)   I. Title.
    BS2555.52.K56   2008
    226'.066—dc22   2008008394

Contents

Figures   vi

Introduction   vii

1. What Is Q?   1

2. Reconstructing a Lost Gospel   41

3. What a Difference Difference Makes   62

4. Q, *Thomas*, and James   98

Appendix: The Sayings Gospel Q in English   123

Glossary   145

Further Readings   149

Notes   153

Index   165

Figures

1. Accounting for the Medial Character of Mark   7

2. A Simple Branch   15

3. The Two Document Hypothesis   16

4. Matthew-Luke Agreements in Placing
   the Double Tradition   18

5. The Two Gospel ("Griesbach") Hypothesis   23

6. "Mark without Q" Hypothesis   29

7. Models of Transmission of the Jesus Tradition   39

Introduction

The idea of a collection of sayings of Jesus lying behind the Gospels of Matthew and Luke is not a new idea. Predecessors of the modern notion of Q have been part of scholarship for two centuries now. Yet only recently has the Sayings Gospel Q come to figure in our reconstructions of Christian origins and to make a real difference in how Christian origins are imagined.

Throughout much of the twentieth century, the Two Document hypothesis—the Synoptic hypothesis that posits Q—was taken so much for granted that introductions to the New Testament routinely devoted only a few pages to its explanation. It seemed almost a certainty. Alternate hypotheses, if they were considered at all, were often simply brushed aside. Now, thanks to the tireless work of the detractors of the Two Document hypothesis, its defenders have had to work harder and more thoughtfully. Perhaps ironically, the fruit of criticism is that the grounds for supposing that Mark is the earliest of the three Synoptic Gospels, and that Matthew and Luke used a sayings source in constructing their Gospels, are better articulated than ever. The Two Document hypothesis is still a hypothesis, of course. But it is better theorized and defended as a hypothesis.

For almost all of the nineteenth century and most of the twentieth, scholars were satisfied with the idea of a Q but not much invested its reconstruction. Q functioned as a kind of algebraic unknown that helped to solve other problems, such as the extent and nature of Matthean and Lukan editorial tendencies. To be sure, a handful of scholars undertook their own reconstructions—Adolf von Harnack in 1907, Athanasius Polag in 1979, and Wilhelm Schenk in 1981. Although each was the product of impressive erudition, none had a very significant impact, theologically or for the construction of Christian origins. It was not until the mid 1980s that a large project was inaugurated under the auspices of the Society of Biblical Literature to produce a fully documented and collaborative reconstruction of Q. The *Critical Edition of Q* was published in 2000 and Greek-English, Greek-German, and Greek-Spanish versions followed in 2002, making a reconstruction of Q widely available for the first time.[1] This reconstruction is not intended to be the last word in reconstructions of Q, but rather a solid basis on which to continue the discussion. The *Critical Edition* was compiled in conjunction with a full database of all arguments invoked by scholars on the reconstruction Q from 1838 up to the present and published as *Documenta Q*.[2] Scholars may now survey the entire breadth of scholarship on Q, evaluate those arguments, and contribute their own.

One of the most significant developments in the study of Christian origins is the new willingness of scholars to imagine real diversity at the beginnings of the Jesus movement. The discovery of new extracanonical Gospels in the past sixty years—the *Gospel of Thomas*, the *Gospel of Philip*, the *Gospel of the Savior*, the *Gospel of Judas*—has made it clear that the Jesus movement was variegated and diverse, with early Jesus groups constituting themselves around differing sets of traditions, differing ethnocultural identities, and differing ecclesial practices. While the sayings and deeds of Jesus play an extremely small role in Paul's theology, the death and resurrection of Jesus is central to it. Conversely, some Gospels such as the *Gospel of Thomas* feature Jesus' sayings, to the exclusion of almost everything else, including the death and resurrection of Jesus. Salvation, or as *Thomas* puts it, "not tasting death," is connected with finding the correct interpretation of Jesus' sayings, not with participation by faith in the death and resurrection of Jesus, as it was for Paul. Matthew and James claim that keeping the whole Torah is incumbent on Jesus' followers. Paul, by contrast, argued that circumcision, one of the key identity markers for Judeans, was not a requirement for Gentile Christians. Such differences are far from incidental. On the contrary, they go to the heart of the various identities of the Jesus groups. Decisions concerning which traditions to privilege and which practices to embrace created multiple Christianities.

In this newfound willingness to embrace significant diversity the Sayings Gospel Q has found an important place, since it is an instance of a *different kind of Gospel* at the earliest levels of the Jesus tradition. As I will argue in chapter 3, knowing about Q changes much of the way we think about the development of the earliest Gospel-telling. Because Q lacks any direct reference to Jesus' death and resurrection, we can no longer suppose that every literary account of the significance of Jesus had to narrate his death. Moreover, Q, since it is almost certainly from Jewish Palestine, gives us a glimpse of a Gospel formulated by Jesus' Galilean followers, quite different in complexion from the diasporic and Gentile Christianities that we know from other sources.

Finally, recent scholarship on Christian origins has emphasized that the culture of the eastern Mediterranean was oral-scribal. Reading literacy was very low, which meant that most of the early Jesus people heard stories and sayings performed orally. Texts were composed by those few competent to write, but texts such as Q were composed to function more like a musical script for performance than a textbook to be read. New understandings of oral-scribal interactions and the ways that traditional texts could be adapted and redeployed orally have helped to answer the longstanding puzzle, What happened to Q?

Q, The Earliest Gospel is intended as an introduction to the Sayings Gospel Q, treating four basic questions: Why should we think there was a Q? What did Q look like? What difference does Q make? And what happened to Q? Naturally, the curious will want to read more, and there is much more to read on each of these questions.[3]

A few readers' notes:

First, it is now customary to refer to Q texts by their *Lukan* versification. Thus, Q 6:20 is the Q text that is found at Luke 6:20. This designation, however, does not necessarily imply that Luke's wording represents the wording of Q, or that Luke's relative placement of Q 6:20 reflects the original sequence of Q (although it is generally thought that in Luke the sequence of Q sayings is less altered than in Matthew). In the few instances where Matthew alone may have preserved a Q text, the designation Q/Matt is used (e.g., Q/Matt. 5:43 as the Q text that underlies Matt. 5:43).

Second, I use the term "Judean," as a noun and an adjective to designate persons of Jewish Palestine in antiquity. This avoids problematic aspects of the English term "Jew" and "Jewish," which has come to refer to Jews only insofar as they were religious. The terms *Ioudaios* and *Ioudaikos*, by contrast, were ethnic-geographical designators, like Egyptian, Phrygian, or Phoenician. They refer to persons identified with a certain cultural region (Judea), whether or not they currently reside in Judea, the Galilee, or the Diaspora. Of course *Ioudaioi* would be likely to observe "Judean" customs and to reverence their ancestral god. The term, however, does not have their beliefs or cult exclusively or necessarily in view, but includes a range of features of ethnic identity.

Third, the appendix prints an English translation of the *Critical Edition of Q*. I have modified the translation in minor ways, and added notes where I found myself in disagreement with my fellow editors, James M. Robison and Paul Hoffmann, on matters of reconstruction.

Existing biblical translations rarely ensure that a phrase or word translated in one way in one Gospel is rendered in the same way in another Gospel, with the result that English translations often convey a misleading impression of where the Gospels agree in wording and where they disagree. For this reason, the translation of biblical texts here has been frequently modified so that the Greek of Matthew, Mark, and Luke is rendered in such a way that the English reflects the agreements and disagreements that exist in Greek.

I am deeply grateful to Philip Law of Westminster John Knox for his kind invitation to write this book and to continue to learn about Q and Christian origins. I dedicate this volume to my many students, undergraduate and graduate. Entering a classroom and embarking on a process of intellectual discovery, mine and theirs, is both a great privilege and a deep satisfaction.

Chapter One

What Is Q?

By the fourth century of the Common Era, Christians had to decide which of their writings should be regarded as authoritative, which were useful but not normative, and which should be rejected as deviant or heretical. This process was necessary, for by that time many Gospels, letters, apocalypses, and sundry treatises existed, each vying for authority within local Christian communities.

For many of these documents, we have only names. But what an assortment of names there are! There were Gospels written under the names of virtually all of the men and women associated with Jesus; apocalypses ascribed to Peter, Paul, and James; acts of Andrew, Peter, Paul, Thomas, John, and Pilate; and letters purporting to come from a host of personages mentioned in the New Testament. Most of these have perished, but a handful survives, mostly in tiny fragments or in brief excerpts quoted by other writers.

Occasionally the sands of Egypt give up one of these lost documents as they did in the 1890s when fragments of the *Gospel of Thomas* were discovered in Upper Egypt and later, in 1945, when Coptic versions of the *Gospel of Thomas*, *Gospel of Philip*, the *First* and *Second Apocalypses of James* and many other extracanonical documents were found. More often, we must reconstruct the contents of these lost documents through a careful analysis of the later documents which quoted or referred to them, as we must do in the case of Paul's original letter to the Corinthians. This is what must be done in the case of the Sayings Gospel Q.

Q is neither a mysterious papyrus nor a parchment from stacks of uncataloged manuscripts in an old European library. It is a document whose existence we must assume in order to make sense of other features of the Gospels. Although the siglum Q seems rather mysterious and the idea of a lost Gospel sounds like it comes from the plot of a modern thriller, the truth is a little more banal. "Q" is a shorthand for the German word *Quelle*, meaning "source." Scholars did not invent Q out of a fascination for mysterious or lost documents. Q is posited from logical necessity.

Put simply, the most efficient and compelling way to explain the relationship among the Synoptic Gospels—Matthew, Mark, and Luke—is to assume that Mark was used independently as a source for Matthew and Luke. Matthew and Luke, however, share some material that they did not get from Mark, about 4,500 words. It is this material that makes up the bulk of Q. It may be that some day we will have more tangible evidence of Q—perhaps a papyrus fragment of this document or other early documents that quoted Q. For now, however, we must rely on what can be deduced about this document from the two Gospels which used it, Matthew and Luke. This chapter will explain the reasons for positing Q. It begins with some observations about the Synoptic Gospels.

A Literary Relationship among the Gospels

Comparison of the Synoptic Gospels indicates that some sort of *literary* relationship exists among them. Put simply, two have copied from the other, or one has copied from the other two.

There are several reasons for this conclusion. First, the first three Gospels often display a high degree of verbatim agreement. Compare, for example, the stories of Jesus calling the four fishermen (Matt. 4:18–22 || Mark 1:16–20). The strong verbal agreement is obvious. In Greek, Matthew's pericope contains eighty-nine words;

Mark has eighty-two. They agree on fifty-seven or 64 percent of Matthew's words and 69.5 percent of Mark's (the word count in English will differ a bit). This degree of verbal agreement is at least as high as in other instances where we know one author to be copying another.

The agreements are significant, since they include not only the memorable saying, "Follow me and I will make you fishers of men," which might be memorized, but also the rather unnecessary explanation, "for they were fishermen." Moreover, Matthew and Mark agree even on very small details, for example, the *type* of net that was used. Matthew calls it an *amphibalestron*, a circular casting net and only one of the several types of nets in use in the first century CE. Mark uses the cognate verb, *amphiballein*. Both agree in mentioning the father of James and John even though he, like Mark's hired help, plays no special role in the story.

The agreements between Matthew and Mark do not extend simply to choice of words, but include the order of episodes. Both accounts name Simon first, then Andrew, then James, then John, even though other lists of these disciples—Mark 3:16–18; 13:3 and the *Gospel of the Ebionites*, for example—name these disciples in a different order. There is no special reason for narrating the call of Peter and Andrew first, and only then James and John; yet Matthew and Mark agree on this sequence. In the Gospel of John, by contrast, Andrew comes first, then Peter, and James and John are not mentioned at all (John 1:35–42). Hence, the agreement of Matthew with Mark to narrate the call of the four disciples in the same order, and in the same way, agreeing on various minor details, points to *literary dependence*: one has copied the other, or both have copied a common source.

Similar observations could be made of pericopae that Luke has in common with Mark. Take, for example, the call of Levi, Mark 2:13–14 and Luke 5:27–28. Mark has thirty-six words in Greek, Luke has twenty-four, but they agree on sixteen of those words or two-thirds of Luke's words. What is perhaps most remarkable is that the call of Levi is narrated at all. Levi appears only here in known Gospel tradition; he is never mentioned again by any other source. (Matthew changed the name to "Matthew," probably to connect this disciple with the one named in Matt. 10:3 || Mark 3:18). That Mark and Luke would choose to relate the call of so obscure a disciple, both putting this call immediately after the story of the cure of the paralytic (Mark 2:1–12 || Luke 5:17–26) suggests that one account has borrowed from the other, or that both are using a common source.

Finally, we can compare Matthew and Luke and again find instances of very strong verbal agreement. Take, for example, John the Baptist's address to the crowds (Matt. 3:7–10 || Luke 3:7–9). The agreement between Matthew and Luke is remarkable: Matthew has seventy-six words in Greek, sixty-one or 80 percent in agreement with Luke. Luke has seventy-two words, sixty-one or 85 percent agreeing exactly with Matthew. Although there are slightly differing introductions, the words of John are virtually identical, apart from Matthew's singular noun "fruit" and its dependent adjective "worthy" in place of Luke's plural noun and adjective. Matthew has "do not presume" in contrast to Luke's "do not begin." Luke also has an extra *kai* in verse 9 which is not easily translatable in English but is used for emphasis.

This type of agreement includes not only the choice of vocabulary, but extends to the inflection of words, word order, and the use of particles—the most variable aspects of Greek syntax. If Matthew and Luke were reproducing this oracle freely from memory, it is most unlikely that they would agree so closely on such highly variable elements of Greek. This type of agreement can be explained only on the supposition that Matthew copied Luke or vice versa, or both used a common written source.

There is yet another reason to think that the Synoptics are related through literary copying. If we align the three Gospels in parallel columns, as is done in modern synopses such as Kurt Aland's *Synopsis of the Four Gospels* or Burton Throckmorton's *Gospel Parallels*,[1] we see that the three often agree in relating the same incidents in the same relative order.

Although in the early part of Matthew (3–13), Matthew and Mark have a rather different order of events, from Matthew 14:1

and Mark 6:16 onward the two Gospels agree almost completely in sequence. The significance of this strong agreement cannot be missed. If Matthew and Mark were completely independent tellings of the story of Jesus, it is unlikely that the writers would choose to relate all stories and sayings in the same order, especially when there was no thematic or narrative reason to do so. For example, there is no special reason why the story of Jesus' argument with the Pharisees about washing hands (Matt. 15:1–20 || Mark 7:1–23) should appear just before the story of the Syro-Phoenician woman's daughter (Matt. 15:21–28 || Mark 7:24–30), or why the controversies about payment of taxes (Matt. 22:15–22 || Mark 12:13–17) comes just before the controversy about the resurrection (Matt. 22:23–33 || Mark 12:18–27). Yet Matthew and Mark agree in these sequences and in many more pericopae. Luke and Mark agree in sequence even more strongly than do Matthew and Mark, and this indicates that copying has occurred.

Thus, we can conclude that *some kind of literary relationship exists among the first three Gospels.* At this point we cannot decide who is copying whom, but it is clear that both the wording and the sequence of the three Gospels is the result of literary interaction.

Mark as the Earliest Gospel

Mark is usually treated as the earliest of the three Gospels and thought to have served as a literary source for Matthew and Luke. There are two steps in arriving at this conclusion.

Mark as Medial

Let us begin with the materials in the Synoptics where Matthew, Mark, and Luke have parallel stories. While Matthew often agrees with Mark's wording of a story or saying, and while Luke often agrees with Mark's wording, it is relatively rare to find Matthew and Luke agreeing *when Mark has a different wording.* Take, for example, the story of the healing of Simon's mother-in-law in Matthew 8:14–15 || Mark 1:29–31 || Luke 4:38–39:

Matthew 8:14–15	*Mark 1:29–31*	*Luke 4:38–39*
And	**And** <u>immediately</u>, leaving *the synagogue* they came **to** ***the*** ***house*** *of Simon* <u>and</u> <u>Andrew, with James</u> <u>and John.</u>	Now arising from *the synagogue,* he entered *the house of Simon.*
coming **to the house** of Peter, Jesus		
saw his **mother-in-law** ill and *burning with a fever.*	*Now the* **mother-in-law** *of Simon* was lying down, *burning with a fever, and* <u>immediately</u> they are telling him *about her.*	*Now the mother-in-law of Simon* was afflicted with a serious fever, *and* they asked him *about her.*
And he touched **her hand** **and the fever left her, and** being raised **she served** him.	***And*** <u>approaching he</u> <u>raised her up</u> by grasping **her hand**. **And the fever** *left* *her* and *she served* them.	*And* standing over her, he rebuked the fever and it *left her.* Getting up at once *she served them.*

Matthew and Mark agree in much of their wording (in **bold**), and Mark and Luke agree in many details (in *italic*). Matthew and Mark both use a participial construction of a verb, *pyressein*, "to burn with a fever," while Luke uses the related noun *pyretos*, "fever," which Matthew and Luke use later. Matthew and Mark have Jesus heal by touching or grasping the woman's hand and both have the phrase "and the fever left her." Luke mentions "fever" here, but it is the object of the verb "rebuke" rather than the subject of the verb "left."

Mark and Luke also agree, referring to Simon's house and Simon's mother-in-law, and both relate an exchange between Jesus and the disciples "about her." Note by contrast that in Matthew Jesus sees the woman and takes the initiative to heal her without any prompting from the disciples. And while Matthew says that she arose and served *him* (Jesus), Mark and Luke have the women serve all the disciples ("them").

What is important to note here is that Matthew and Luke do not agree with each other *against Mark* in any detail. It is true that Matthew and Luke fail to repeat some of the details in Mark: "immediately" (twice); "and Andrew, with James and John"; and "approaching he raised her up" (underscored). But they do not agree *positively* against Mark.

This pattern, which could be illustrated by reference to other pericopae as well, suggests that the relationship between Matthew and Luke is *indirect* rather than direct. If there had been a direct connection between Matthew and Luke, we should expect Matthew sometimes to agree with Luke against Mark. But agreements of this sort are in fact quite uncommon (although there are some that we shall have to discuss later). The fact that Matthew and Luke tend to agree with Mark, but not against Mark, means that *Mark is medial*. This does not in itself imply that Mark is the earliest of the three, although that is one possibility. In fact several arrangements of the Gospels are possible with Mark as the middle term (see fig. 1).

In each of these arrangements, there is no direct connection between Matthew and Luke, and, hence, no possibility of them

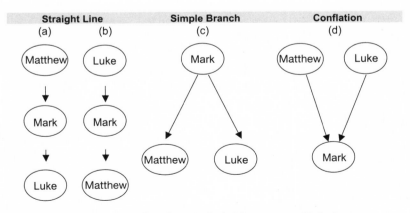

Figure 1. Accounting for the Medial Character of Mark

agreeing with each other apart from Mark, except by coincidence. In the first straight-line arrangement (*a*), if Mark changed Matthew's wording, Luke would not agree with Matthew (except by coincidence), since he has no direct access to Matthew. The same is true in the second straight-line arrangement (*b*): if Mark changed Luke's wording, Matthew could not agree with Luke except coincidentally. Or in the simple branch solution (*c*), in cases where Matthew changes Mark, it would be unexpected to see Luke always changing Mark *in the same way*. If we understand the pericope mentioned above on a simple branch solution, Matthew changed Mark's "Simon" to the more common "Peter." He has Jesus take the initiative in the healing and he adds that Jesus heals by mere touch. Note that Luke lacks *all* of these Matthean changes. On the other hand, Matthew lacks Luke's additions to Mark, the qualification of the fever as "serious" and Jesus rebuking the fever. According to this model, Matthew and Luke independently edited Mark, but cannot agree against Mark, since neither has direct access to the other's work.

The fourth model, conflation (*d*), also accounts for nonagreement against Mark but in a different way. On the first three models, there are no Matthew-Luke agreements against Mark because Matthew and Luke are not in direct contact. In the conflation model, Mark *chooses* not to disagree with Matthew and Luke when he sees them in agreement. In the pericope above, Mark saw that both Matthew and Luke had "to the house," "mother-in-law," and "she served" and so reproduced this agreement. But where Matthew and Luke had different wording, Mark sometimes sided with Matthew, taking over the entire phrase "and the fever left her," but also took over from Luke the mention of a synagogue and the concluding phrase, "she served them." On this model, Mark also added a few details of his own (<u>underscored</u>).

This model is more complicated than the others, since it presupposes that Mark had before him both accounts and moved back and forth between the two, picking elements from one, then the other. Such a model is not logically impossible, but examination of how other authors worked who combined two sources reveals that no known ancient author would have taken the trouble to compare sources so closely and to zigzag between them. An ancient conflator would more likely have taken over Matthew's account or Luke's but not bothered to micro-conflate them.[2]

A second set of data also points to the conclusion that Mark is medial. If we compare the sequence of episodes in each of the Gospels, an important pattern emerges. While Matthew sometimes relates an episode in a different sequence than Mark and Luke, and while Luke sometimes relates an episode in a different sequence than Mark and Matthew, *Matthew and Luke never agree in locating an episode differently from Mark's sequence.*

When, for example, Matthew relocates a Markan episode such as Mark 5:1–20, the exorcism of a demoniac, to an entirely new location (Matt. 8:28–34), Luke agrees with Mark, not Matthew. There is only one episode in the Synoptics where both relocate a text of Mark (3:13–19), but they do so to *different* locations, Matthew moving it to a point before Mark 2:23–3:12 (‖ Matt. 12:1–16), a series of controversy stories, while Luke simply inverts the order of Mark 3:7–12 and 3:13–19 so that the naming of the Twelve comes before a list of the various peoples that came to see Jesus. That is, even where both Matthew and Luke disagree with Mark's sequence, they also disagree with each other.

These data reinforce the earlier conclusion: Mark is medial. In matters of sequence, we find Matthew agreeing with Mark's order, and Luke agreeing with Mark's order, but we never find Matthew and Luke agreeing to place a story where Mark has an entirely different placement. This datum suggests that there is no direct relationship between Matthew and Luke. Any of the possible arrangements of three Gospels indicated in figure 1 might account for these data.

How, then, do scholars conclude that Mark is the earliest of the three, that is, that we should think of the relationship among the Synoptics as a "simple branch solution"? The conclusion follows from detailed comparisons of Mark with Matthew and Mark with Luke.

From Medial Mark to Prior Mark

Several kinds of considerations suggest that Mark is the earliest of the three Synoptics.

One reason for considering Mark as prior to Matthew and Luke rather than dependent on one or both of these gospels has to do with assessing Mark's omissions. If Mark knew and used Matthew (either *a* or *d* in fig. 1), he must also have omitted a number of Matthean pericopae, including the account of Jesus' birth, the Sermon on the Mount, many parables, and especially the account of Jesus' appearance to his disciples after his death. The latter omission would be particularly awkward to explain, since Mark repetitively has Jesus predict his resurrection (Mark 8:31; 9:9, 31; 10:32–34) and even has him declare that he will meet his disciples in the Galilee (14:27), which is precisely where Matthew's Jesus appears (Matt. 28:16–20). Mark, however, famously ends his Gospel with the women at the tomb "not telling anyone anything for they were afraid" (16:8)—an ending that reverses Matthew's conclusion, where Jesus commands the women to tell his "brothers" that they will see him in the Galilee, which the reader must assume happened, since the disciples see Jesus on a mountain in the Galilee (28:16–20).

Likewise, if Mark knew Luke—either *b* or *d* in figure 1—he must also have omitted Luke's infancy stories, the sermon at Nazareth (Luke 4:16–30), the Sermon on the Plain, many of Luke's parables and sayings found in Luke 9:51–18:15, and the resurrection appearances. It is perhaps imaginable that Mark might have omitted Luke's appearance stories, since they are all centered on Jerusalem, not the Galilee. But why omit the account of Jesus' birth and childhood? Johann Jakob Griesbach, who thought that Mark used and condensed both Matthew and Luke, suggested that Mark was silent about the infancy of Jesus because he wished to concentrate on Jesus as a teacher.[3] But this explanation will hardly do, since Luke's repeated motif of the young Jesus growing in wisdom (2:40, 52) and his story of Jesus debating with the scribes at the age of twelve (2:41–52) function precisely to demonstrate that Jesus' teaching abilities were manifest from a very young age. That is, Luke's infancy story serves to underscore a major Markan theme and hence it is difficult to conclude that Mark would have omitted it if he knew Luke's account.

Second, to see Mark as later than Matthew and Luke raises some grave difficulties regarding the depiction of Jesus' family. As is well known, Matthew makes clear that Joseph was told about the identity of Jesus by an angel (Matt. 1:20–21), and Luke describes Mary as understanding the wondrous events surrounding Jesus' birth and childhood (Luke 2:19, 51). (Note again that while both Matthew and Luke treat Jesus' family as positively disposed to him, they do so *differently*, another sign of the independence of Matthew and Luke.) Yet Mark treats Jesus' family as opposed to him and as unknowing: they attempt to seize him on the belief that he is insane (Mark 3:20–21), an episode which both Matthew and Luke omit. Mark also relates the story of Jesus' family wanting to speak with him and Jesus' response: he points to the crowd of disciples with the words, "See, my mother and my brothers; whoever does the will of God is my brother and sister and mother" (Mark 3:34–35). Given Mark's context, this can only function as a rejection of Jesus' birth family.

Mark's treatment of Jesus' family is negative whether or not he had Matthew or Luke in front of him. But if Mark used either Matthew or Luke or both as sources, his inversion of their positive representations of Jesus' kin is remarkable, and does not correspond to any other known representation of Jesus' family in the early church, which, as time went on, viewed Jesus' kin more and more positively. The likeliest scenario is that rather than Mark inverting a positive depiction of Jesus' family in his source(s), Matthew and Luke are undoing Mark's critical perspective on Jesus' family.

Finally, when we compare Mark with Matthew and Mark with Luke, it is clear that in general Matthew's and Luke's version of Mark's stories are improved, both grammatically and in terms of their content. Throughout, where Mark displays the excessive use of "and" to join clauses, Matthew uses an array of subordinating conjunctions, participial phrases, or other devices to arrive at a better-flowing style. Matthew also eliminates certain problematic expressions in Mark. For example, at Matthew 13:58 he has "and [Jesus] did not perform many mighty deeds there because of their unbelief" where Mark 6:5–6 has "and [Jesus] *could not* perform any mighty deeds there except that he laid his hands on a few sick persons and healed them; and he marveled at their unbelief."

Matthew's version avoids the inference that Jesus, a powerful wonder worker, was somehow unable to perform miracles. On the contrary, it was the lack of faith that Jesus encountered in his hometown which inclined Jesus not to perform many wonders.

Similar observations can be made regarding Luke and Mark. Luke's Greek is better than Mark's, with greater use of subordinating conjunctions and better connectives. Luke also emphasizes Jesus' piety (4:16) and prayerfulness to the extent that each key event of Jesus' career—his baptism, the choosing of the disciples, Peter's confession, the transfiguration, Jesus' teaching on prayer, and the visit to Gethsemane—is accompanied by prayer. And in contrast to Mark, the Lukan Jesus dies not with a cry of abandonment, but with a prayer, "into your hands I commend my spirit" (Luke 23:46). These touches are more probably explained as Luke's additions to Mark than they are as Mark's omissions from Luke, for Mark has no reason to downplay Jesus' piety or prayerfulness. Luke clarifies details in Mark, for example, taking over the Markan Jesus' declaration, "I have not come to call the righteous, but sinners" (Mark 2:17), but adding "*to repentance*" (Luke 5:32), thus obviating the objection that Jesus simply liked to associate with evil persons. Features of this sort are better treated as Luke's additions to Mark than as Mark's omissions.

Observations of this kind could be multiplied considerably. The point is that in comparing Matthew with Mark, and Luke with Mark, it is almost always simpler to see Matthew and Luke as transforming Mark than vice versa. This leads us to conclude that of the four scenarios pictured in figure 1, the most likely one is the simple branch (*c*), with Mark serving as the source for Matthew and Luke, who edited Mark and did so in different ways.

The Other Synoptic Source, Q

If Matthew and Luke used Mark independently, we are still left to explain other material common to Matthew and Luke. Matthew and Luke share about 4,500 words that they did not get from Mark. This includes much of the Sermon on the Mount/Sermon on the Plain; the woes against the Pharisees; parables such as the

Yeast, the Faithful and Unfaithful Servant, the Great Supper, and the Entrusted Money; and sayings such as the Lord's Prayer and the warning about serving God or mammon. Let us call this material the "double tradition."

Just as I have argued with respect to the sayings and stories that Matthew and Luke share with Mark, with the double tradition too we must assume some kind of *literary relationship*. Comparison of Matthew and Luke shows that the verbatim agreement in the double tradition ranges from 96 percent to less than 10 percent. In a significant number of pericopae the agreement is so high that it is impossible to suppose that Matthew and Luke have coincidentally taken over bits of oral tradition, adding these to Mark. They must have used a common document. Take, for instance, the woes against the Galilean cities (Matt. 11:20–24 and Luke 10:13–15).

Although Matthew has an introduction unparalleled in Luke, the words of the oracle itself correspond closely: Jesus' speech comprises seventy-eight words in Matthew and forty-six in Luke, forty-five of them identical with Matthew. As I remarked earlier a propos of Matthew 3:7–10 || Luke 3:7–9, agreements are not only vocabularic but in the sequence of words. Both Matthew and Luke have the sequence "but / for Tyre and Sidon / more tolerable / it shall be / than for you." Had Matthew and Luke known this saying only via oral performances, we would expect not only greater differences in vocabulary, but also variation in word order—for example, "but / it shall be / more tolerable / for Tyre and Sidon / than for you," or "but / more tolerable / it shall be / for Tyre and Sidon / than for you." Since Greek, unlike English, allows for sentence parts to come in many different sequences without a loss of meaning, Matthew and Luke's agreement is highly significant: the two agree on vocabulary *and* on verbal sequence. This kind of agreement is only intelligible if there is a direct or indirect literary relationship between the two.

Even where Matthew does not have as high a level of agreement with Luke, it is still clear that a common source is being used. For example, both Matthew and Luke have Jesus warn of coming divisions:

³⁴*Do not* suppose *that* I have come to cast *peace* upon *earth*; I have not come to cast peace, *but* a sword. ³⁵*For* I have come to set a man against his *father, and a daughter* against her *mother*, and *a daughter-in-law* against her *mother-in-law*; ³⁶and a person's enemies will be those of his own household. (Matt. 10:34–36)

⁵¹Do you think *that* I am here to give *peace* on *earth*? No, I tell you, *but* rather division; ⁵²*for* henceforth in one house there will be five divided, three against two and two against three; ⁵³they will be divided, father against son and son against *father*, mother against daughter *and daughter* against *mother*, mother-in-law against her daughter-in-law and daughter-in-law against *mother-in-law*. (Luke 12:51–53)

The degree of verbatim agreement is very much lower than in Matthew 11:20–24 || Luke 10:13–15 cited above. It is nonetheless likely that Matthew and Luke are citing the same saying and that one or both have adjusted its wording. They agree on the basic structure of the saying: "do not suppose that . . . but . . . ," then a rationale introduced by "for," and finally an illustration of divisions by reference to a household. Matthew's version uses more visual language: he speaks of "casting" or "throwing" (*balein*) peace, as if peace were a substance that can be thrown like seeds. Luke by contrast uses the more abstract term "division." Nevertheless, Matthew and Luke—and hence, their source—agree in treating division as epitomized in *household division*. This is a significant agreement, since divisions might just as easily have been illustrated by feuds between neighbors, or among clans, or between villages, or battles between kingdoms. Furthermore, both imagine a *patrilocal* Palestinian marriage, where the wife comes to live with her husband's kin, so that mothers-in-law and daughters-in-law are in the same house.

Thus, even when verbal agreement is quite low—and this pericope has the third-lowest verbal agreement of any in the double tradition⁴—there are still strong grounds for concluding that Matthew and Luke had a common source and modified it to fit their literary tastes.

If the materials which Matthew and Luke have in common and which are not present in Mark are related literarily, how should we imagine that relationship? We have already excluded any arrangement of the three Gospels that puts Matthew in direct contact with Luke, since in that case one would expect to find instances where Matthew agrees with Luke's sequence against Mark, and we do not find any such agreements. And we would expect, for example, Luke to have some of the same additions to Mark that Matthew made, or for Matthew to have adopted some of Luke's additions to Mark. The fact that Matthew and Luke lack each other's major modifications to Mark suggests that they have not seen each other's work.

This leaves as the simplest solution a second, simple branch solution, like Mark's relationship to Matthew and Luke, but applying this model to the double tradition.[5] Since we do not know what this document was called, scholars have adopted the siglum "Q," from the German word *Quelle*, "source" (see fig. 2).

If we then combine the Markan simple branch with the Q simple branch, we arrive at what scholars call the Two Document (2DH) or Two Source hypothesis, the two "documents" being Mark and Q (see fig. 3).

This arrangement makes sense of three key data sets.

1. The Two Document hypothesis makes sense of the fact that Matthew and Luke tend not to agree with each other against Mark in the wording of stories that Mark has. This is because each edits Mark independently and hence usually edits Mark in different ways.[6] And although both Matthew and Luke sometimes relocate

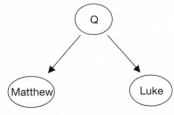

Figure 2. A Simple Branch

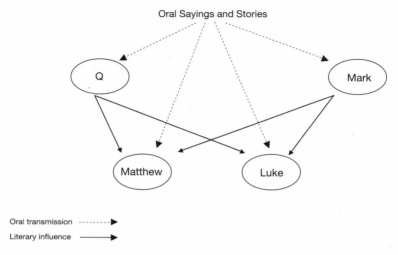

Figure 3. The Two Document Hypothesis

Markan stories or sayings to new locations, they never move the same story to the same non-Markan location.

2. The second set of data concerns the Q material. While there is often a high degree of verbal agreement between Matthew and Luke within these sections, there is practically *no agreement* in the placement of these sayings relative to Mark. Matthew places his Beatitudes after the Markan story of the four fishermen (Matt. 4:18–22 ‖ Mark 1:16–20, 21) or Mark's description of Jesus' preaching tour through the Galilee (Matt 4:23 ‖ Mark 1:39), depending upon how Synoptic tables are aligned. Luke, however, inserted the Beatitudes following the Markan story of the healing of the man with the withered hand (Luke 6:6–11 ‖ Mark 3:1–6) and the naming of the Twelve (Luke 6:12–16 ‖ Mark 3:13–19). Matthew used the woes against the Galilean towns as part of Jesus' attack on "this generation's" rejection of John the Baptist and Jesus (Matt. 11:2–30); in Luke they form part of the commissioning speech directed to the seventy-two disciples (Luke 10:1–16). Similarly, Matthew used the saying on serving two masters in the middle of his Sermon on the Mount (Matt. 6:24), while in Luke it appears two-thirds of the way through his Gospel after the para-

ble of the Unjust Steward and various sayings concerning money and greed (Luke 16:1–13). There is, in other words, nothing to suggest that Matthew was influenced by Luke's placement of the Q material or vice versa. Had there been a direct relationship between Matthew and Luke—Luke using Matthew or Matthew using Luke—one would expect Matthew's placement of the Q material relative to Mark to have influenced Luke's editorial choices or vice versa.

There are only three pericopae—all related—where Matthew and Luke agree on placing the Q material in the *same* relative position, in the opening section of Matthew and Luke dealing with John the Baptist and Jesus' temptation (see fig. 4).

In all three cases (Q 3:3, 7b–9; 3:16–17; 4:1–13) the Q material overlapped Mark in content. John's preaching of repentance in Q (3:7b–9) contained an introduction to John's oracle (Q 3:3, 7a) which overlapped Mark 1:2–6; both Mark and Q contained a version of the prediction of the Coming/Stronger One, although Q's version (Q 3:16–17) was longer than Mark's (Mark 1:7–8); and both Q and Mark had a testing story, Mark's being only two verses long (1:12–13), while Q had an elaborate three-part test (Q 4:1–13). Naturally, Matthew and Luke attached the Q saying regarding John's preaching to the same Markan pericope (Mark 1:2–6) because there Mark is also describing John's preaching. Similarly, Mark's version of John's prediction of the "Stronger One" (Mark 1:7–8) was the obvious point at which to use Q's longer prediction of the Coming One and his eschatological activities (Q 3:16–17). Finally, Mark's short account of Jesus' temptation (Mark 1:12–13) is virtually the only place at which Matthew and Luke could have used Q's longer and more elaborate temptation account (Q 4:1–13). But after this point in Mark, Matthew and Luke are consistent in *not* placing Q material in the same place relative to Mark. This is explicable if Matthew and Luke were not in direct contact—neither had seen how the other had connected Mark and Q.

Consider the imaginary scenario of having two documents, one a narrative about a hero, and the other a collection of the hero's sayings and speeches. If you were to give these two documents to five

Q	Matthew	Mark	Luke	Q
3:3 ⇒ John in the Wilderness	*3:1–6* (Q+Mk)	⇐ 1:2–6 ⇒ John in the Wilderness	3:1–7a (Q+Mk)	⇐ 3:3 John in the Wilderness
	3:7a			
3:7b–9 ⇒ Preaching of Repentance	*3:7b–10* (Q)		*3:7b–9* (Q)	⇐ 3:7b–9 Preaching of Repentance
			3:10–15	
3:16 ⇒ Announcement of the Coming One	*3:11* (Q+Mk)	⇐ 1:7–8 ⇒ Announcement of the Coming One	*3:16* (Q+Mk)	⇐ 3:16 Announcement of the Coming One
3:17 ⇒	*3:12 (Q)*		*3:17 (Q)*	⇐ 3:17
			3:18–20	
	3:13–17	⇐ 1:9–11 ⇒ Jesus' Baptism	3:21–22	
			3:23–38	
4:1–2 ⇒ The Testing of Jesus (setting)	*4:1–2* (Q+Mk)	⇐ 1:12–13a ⇒ The Testing of Jesus	*4:1–2* (Q+Mk)	⇐ 4:1–2 The Testing of Jesus (setting)
4:3–13 ⇒ 3 Challenges by the Devil	*4:3–11a (Q)*		*4:3–13 (Q)*	⇐ 4:3–13 3 Challenges by the Devil
	4:11b	⇐ 1:13b Conclusion: The angels appear		

Sigla

3:7b–10	Agreement of Matt. and Luke in placing double tradition material
3:1–6	Overlap of Mark and Q
3:10–15	Special material or editorial additions
1:7–8	Markan material

Figure 4. Matthew-Luke Agreements in Placing the Double Tradition

students, asking them to produce a single narrative document that combined the two sources, stipulating that they could not work together, they would likely produce five *different* combinations of the two documents. This is what has happened with Matthew and Luke.

3. Third, if one does not measure sequential agreement of the Q materials in Matthew and Luke relative to Mark, but relative to each other, approximately one-third of the pericopae, accounting for almost one-half of the word count, are in the same relative order. That is, in spite of the fact that Matthew and Luke place the Q material differently *relative to Mark*, they nonetheless agree in using many of the sayings and stories in the

same order *relative to each other*. Imagine aligning Matthew and Luke in parallel columns and then removing all of the sayings and stories that they took over from Mark (and hence, all of the points at which Q material was attached to the Markan outline). What would result is a set of Q sayings that appear in the *same relative order*.

The sequential agreement that exists between Matthew and Luke's double tradition—thirty-five of the ninety-two pericopae of the double tradition, or about 40 percent—suggests strongly that even if Matthew and Luke were not in direct contact with each other, something influenced their arrangement of the material included in the double tradition. Of course both Matthew and Luke apparently felt free to relocate Q sayings to other locations, just as they did with Mark stories. But the extent of their agreement

Table 1. Sequential Agreements of Matthew and Luke in reproducing the Q material

Matthew	Luke	Matthew	Luke
3:3	3:3	11:16–19	7:31–35
3:7–10	3:7–9	11:20–24	10:13–15
3:11–12	3:16b–17	11:25–26	10:21
4:1–11	4:1–13	11:27	11:22
4:13	4:16a	12:22–28	11:14–20
5:3–4, 6	6:6:20b–21	12:29	11:21–22
5:11–12	6:22–23	12:30	11:23
5:39–42	6:29–30	12:38–40	11:29–30
5:45–47	6:32–35	12:41–42	11:31–32
5:48	6:36	13:31–32	13:18–19
7:1–2	6:37–38	13:33	13:20–21
7:3–5	6:41–42	18:12–14	15:4–7
7:16–20	6:43–44	18:15–22	17:3b–4
7:21	6:46	24:26–28	17:23–24
7:24–27	6:47–49	24:37–39	17:26–27
8:5–10, 13	7:1–10	24:40–41	17:34–35
11:2–6	7:18–23	25:14–30	19:12–26
11:7–11	7:24–48		

suggests that Q is not just a set of oral traditions, which do not have any intrinsic order, but a written document, whose sequence strongly influenced Matthew and Luke's reproduction of it.

It must be reiterated at this point that scholars have not invented Q out of an interest in multiplying sources, or because they are fascinated with mysterious and lost documents. On the contrary, the positing of Q is purely a function of conclusions about the relationship of Matthew and Luke to Mark. Observations of the patterns of agreements and disagreements in wording and in sequence among the Gospels indicates that Mark occupies a medial position between Matthew and Luke; careful comparison of Mark to Matthew and Mark to Luke suggests that Mark is not only medial, but *prior* to Matthew and Luke, and served as one of their sources. But if this is the case, then it is necessary to account for the double tradition (or Q) material that Matthew and Luke share, which they did not take from Mark. If Matthew and Luke were not in direct contact with each other for the Markan material, they cannot very well have been in direct contract for the Q material. This leaves only one viable possibility, that the double tradition material comes from another source, parallel to Mark insofar as it was also a source for Matthew and Luke, used independently by each.

Challenges to the Two Document Hypothesis

Is this the only way to explain the relationship of the Synoptics? Certainly not. Two main alternates have been proposed, the Two Gospel hypothesis (2GH or Griesbach hypothesis), and the Mark without Q hypothesis (MwQH or Farrer-Goulder hypothesis). Before I discuss these alternatives it should be underscored that the Two Document hypothesis, as well as these alternates, are all *hypotheses*: they are scholarly scenarios developed to account for data. None of them has been proved. The fact that the majority of specialists favor the Two Document hypothesis does not make it any less of a hypothesis.

There are two aspects to a good hypothesis. First, it must pay attention to the relevant data to be explained: the facts that Matthew and Luke do not agree with each other against Mark in placing a Markan pericope; that in general Matthew and Luke do not agree against Mark in the wording of a Markan pericope; that in the double tradition Matthew and Luke often register very high verbal agreements, but after Matthew 4:13 do not agree *at all* in the location of the Q material relative to Mark. Every good Synoptic theory must take these data into account.

The second aspect of a good theory is the explanatory "narrative" or the "cover story" that is supplied to make sense of the model. This is like a lawyer's account of the facts of the case—a narrative that tries to incorporate all of the pertinent data into a coherent story. Of course, an opposing lawyer will have a different narrative to account for the same facts.

A good hypothesis is one that accounts for most of the data, most of the time, by the most probable kinds of explanatory mechanisms. A good hypothesis will try to incorporate as much of the data as possible into its narrative. It will attempt to supply a credible account of the Gospel writers' editorial and conceptual procedures. Thus, the Two Document hypothesis proposes that Matthew and Luke have independently used Mark and Q; they have improved Mark's grammar; they both eliminated potential difficulties in Mark's account, for example the inference that Mark's Jesus *could not* do any miracles in Nazareth (Mark 6:5). To say that Matthew improved Mark's grammar is not itself data; that is an *explanation* of data which already presupposes that Matthew used Mark. We might think it a plausible explanation. And we might conclude that it is more plausible than the reverse, that Mark saw Matthew's good grammar and changed it for the worse. Such explanations are cover stories, not data, and certainly not proof.

Most of the debate that occurs among scholars of Synoptic relationships in fact has to do with proposing credible cover stories to explain the data. No hypothesis is without its difficulties, and for any of the existing Synoptic hypotheses there are sets of data which the hypothesis does not explain very well. This is not unique to the study of Synoptic relationships; it is a feature of virtually all hypotheses in the human and experimental sciences. Hence, there is always room both for supplementation and for alternates. What we aim at is a good hypothesis that accounts for as much of the data as possible, and which has explanatory force. That is, it delivers a generally credible picture of Gospel origins.

The Two Gospel Hypothesis

First proposed by Englishman Henry Owen in 1764[7] and popularized by the great German text critic Johann Jakob Griesbach in 1789,[8] the Two Gospel hypothesis (2GH) treats Mark as a conflation of Matthew and Luke (*d* in fig. 1). Griesbach also thought that Luke used Matthew directly (see fig. 5).

Griesbach was impressed by two facts: that the content of Mark's Gospel could be found almost completely in Matthew and Luke, and that Mark seemed alternately to follow Matthew, then Luke's order of pericopae. (This is another way of saying that Matthew and Luke do not agree against Mark in matters of sequence.) In order to make sense of these data, Griesbach proposed a cover story: Mark was a conflation of Matthew and Luke rather than an independent work of Gospel writing. When Mark saw Matthew and Luke in agreement in wording or order he naturally took over that consensus. For this reason there are no disagreements of Mark with the order of Matthew and Luke and relatively few disagreements in wording. But when Mark saw Matthew and Luke with differing sequences or wordings, he sometimes sided with Matthew and sometimes sided with Luke. Hence, Mark zigzags between the other two Gospels.

This scenario accounts for key Synoptic data. But does it account for the data in a plausible fashion? If Mark did not feel free to depart from a Matthew-Luke consensus, why did he not then take over such texts as Matthew 3:7–10 || Luke 3:7–9 or Matthew 11:20–24 || Luke 10:13–15, where Matthew and Luke are in almost perfect agreement? Here proponents of the 2DH must invoke other explanations.

Griesbach suggested that Mark omitted portions of Matthew and Luke that did not pertain to Jesus as a teacher, for example, the Matthaean and Lukan infancy stories.[9] As I have indicated above, this turns out to be a poor explanation, since Luke's infancy

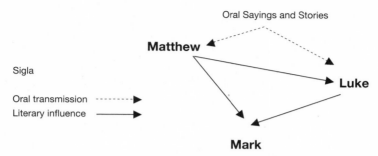

Figure 5. The Two Gospel (Griesbach) Hypothesis

story is constructed to show precisely how Jesus came to be so great a teacher! And if Mark wished to concentrate on Jesus as a teacher, then one might expect him to take over the long speeches of Matthew or Luke, which make up a significant portion of Matthew and which account for about one-third of Luke. But here Griesbach argued that Mark "wanted to write a book of small compass" and so omitted much of Matthew and Luke.[10] So, curiously, Griesbach's Mark wished to highlight Jesus as a teacher, produced a Gospel in which Jesus is repeatedly depicted as teaching, but in which we hear very little of Jesus' actual teaching, apart from some parables in chapter 4 and a few scattered sayings.

Mark's omission of the Sermon on the Mount is a particular problem for the 2GH. William Farmer suggested that Mark followed Matthew's Gospel up to the beginning of the Sermon on the Mount (Matt. 4:23) and then moved over to Luke, following his outline up to just before the beginning of Luke's Sermon on the Plain (Luke 6:12–16). When he moved back to the comparable point in Matthew, he was already at Matthew 12:22 and so had passed over both versions of the sermon.[11] But this does not provide a very satisfactory explanation of the choice to omit either sermon, since it seems to make the omission of the sermon a matter of Mark inadvertently and rather mechanically missing Matthean and Lukan material as he shifted from one source to another. Did not Mark notice that he had omitted both sermons?

Another explanation of the omission has been offered. David Peabody suggests that at Mark 1:21 (Matt. 4:23 || Luke 4:16) Mark's sources had two different sermons, Matthew's Sermon on the Mount (Matt. 4:24–7:29) and Luke's inaugural sermon in Nazareth (Luke 4:16–30). Because they differed so markedly, Mark decided to omit both, noting only that Jesus was teaching in a synagogue (Mark 1:21–22).[12] Then, when Mark reached Luke's Sermon on the Plain he simply passed over it. This, too, is not a very convincing explanation of Mark's preferences, since there are other pericopae where Matthew and Luke differ and where, on the 2GH, Mark simply chose to reproduce one of the two versions.[13] In other words, this is hardly a sufficient explanation of Mark's omission of the two sermons.

Mark Goodacre has rightly criticized Griesbach's solution by observing that while Griesbach was compelled to suppose that Mark omitted the Lord's Prayer, Mark's Gospel is full of themes and phrases redolent of the Lord's Prayer: Mark's Jesus exhorts disciples to pray (11:24–25; 14:38); he addresses God as "Father" (14:36); the Gospel begins with a programmatic assertion that the kingdom is coming (1:14); the doing of God's will is acknowledged as a key aspect of discipleship (3:35); mutual forgiveness is encouraged (11:25); and in Gethsemane Jesus admonishes his disciples to "watch and pray lest they enter into temptation" (14:38; cf. Matt. 6:13 || Luke 11:4).[14] In other words, Mark had every reason to *retain* the Lord's Prayer, so congenial was it to his depiction of Jesus.

I have argued above that there are other difficulties with the 2GH's explanation of Markan omissions. Mark's omission of Jesus' appearance to his disciples after his death is particularly odd, since Mark is so insistent on having Jesus predict his resurrection (Mark 8:31; 9:9, 31; 10:32–34) and even has him predict his reunion with the disciples in the Galilee (14:27). So it is strange that he did not take over Matthew's appearance stories, especially Matthew 28:16–20, which is set in Galilee. Instead, Mark concludes by saying that the women at the tomb were silent about what they had heard (Mark 16:8), which in fact reverses Matthew's ending, where the women expressly tell the other disciples what they saw (Matt. 28:8). Mark's ending also threatens the veracity of

Jesus' prediction in 14:27, since the reader might assume that Mark's disciples were never told of the empty tomb and hence never followed the young man's command to go to Galilee.

Hence, there are some serious explanatory problems with the 2GH. It may be that scholars in the future can posit a different narrative or set of explanations of Mark's Gospel that will prove to be a more satisfactory account of the assumption that he used Matthew and Luke as sources. But so far, no convincing explanation of Mark's omissions has been offered.

A second aspect of the 2GH deserves comment. The 2GH does away with the need to posit Q, since all of the double tradition material in Luke was derived directly from Matthew. This has the great advantage of simplicity: the 2GH does not have to posit a now-lost source lying behind the Synoptics. According to the 2GH, Luke obtained both what we call the Markan material and what we call Q directly from Matthew. His extra stories and sayings—the infancy accounts, some parables, and some of the distinctive portions of his passion and resurrection stories—were presumably from oral traditions he knew. Simplicity, however, has a price.

On the 2GH what we call the Markan and Q materials are connected in one way in Matthew and in a completely different manner in Luke after Matthew 4:13 and Luke 4:16. For example, at Matthew 7:21–27 Matthew has a series of sayings beginning with a warning:

> [21]Not every one who says to me, Lord, Lord, shall enter the kingdom of heaven, but the one who does the will of my Father who is in heaven. [22]On that day many will say to me, "Lord, Lord, did we not prophesy in your name, and cast out demons in your name, and do many mighty works in your name?" [23]And then will I declare to them, "I never knew you; depart from me, you evildoers." [24]Every one then who hears these words of mine and does them will be like a wise man who built his house upon the rock.

The Matthean unit is a well-integrated scene set "on that day," apparently a day of judgment. The Lord speaks to followers who address Jesus as "Lord"—that is, they represent themselves as believers—and also claim to have performed wonders in his name. Nevertheless, the Lord rejects their claims because, despite their wonderworking activities and the title by which they address Jesus, they do not enact the will of God. Hence, they are exposed as false disciples and sent away. The parable of the two builders concluding Matthew's sermon then gives a graphic illustration of the consequences of hearing and doing, and hearing and not doing.

The Two Gospel hypothesis proposes that Luke saw this scene and split it in two, preserving the first and last sayings (Matt. 7:21, 24–27 || Luke 6:46, 47–49) for the Sermon on the Plain, but moving the dialogue with the would-be disciples to chapter 13, where he combined it with another saying pulled out of Matthew's story of the healing of the centurion's serving boy (Matt. 8:5–13). He also changed the sense of Matthew 7:22–23: the persons addressed in Luke 13:26–27 are no longer would-be believers, still less Christian miracle workers, but rather people who were simply acquainted with Jesus, perhaps fellow Galileans: "We ate and drank in your presence, and you taught in our streets."

Why would Luke take the trouble to dismantle Matthew's judgment scene, and why would he then take parts of Matthew's miracle story in 8:5–13 to reassemble them in 13:24–28? This unit is scarcely as coherent a unit as Matthew 7:21–27. Luke begins with a saying about a *narrow* door (13:24) which the addressees are encouraged to strive to get through, but then Luke shifts to a saying about a *closed* door, where people are barred from entry into a house (13:26–27), and concludes with a scene apparently set in the afterlife or the judgment, where the damned are *thrown out* of a house. Luke 13:24 appears to be a general exhortation to moral exertion; verses 25–27 warn those who assume that familial or ethnic associations with Jesus will avail in the judgment, and verses 28–29 visualize the judgment or the afterlife as a recognition scene where Jesus' compatriots find themselves excluded from an eschatological banquet. In other words, Luke's composition seems much less well integrated than Matthew 7:21–27. This then raises the question, why would Luke dismantle a well-constructed scene in order to construct something less coherent?[15]

On the Two Document hypothesis, by contrast, it is Matthew who has reorganized Q (as he has also done with Mark) to arrive at a powerful scene with which to conclude his sermon. Matthew saw two Q texts that were useful for his sermon: Q 6:46–49, which contained the "Lord Lord" saying and the parable of the Builders, and Q 13:25–28, which is a cluster of sayings including the "narrow gate" (Q 13:25), the story of the householder and the closed door (Q 13:26–27), and the prediction of a pilgrimage of foreigners (Q 13:28–29). Matthew saw that the parable of the householder (Q 13:26–27), whose fit in Q 13 was not particularly good, could be integrated into a judgment scene (Matt. 7:21–27). He also saw how the prediction of foreigners coming to sit with the patriarchs (Q 13:28–29) could serve as a fitting saying for Jesus to pronounce at the end of the story of the healing of the Roman centurion's son (Matt. 8:5–13), the first foreigner in Matthew's Gospel to be healed.

What I have just offered is not evidence or proof for the 2DH but rather a scenario of how Matthew operated on the *assumption* that he used Q. The key difference between this scenario and that implied by the 2GH is that on the 2DH we see a movement from less coherent to more coherent units, from less organization to greater and more sophisticated organization. The 2GH must imagine a well-constructed Matthean unit being disassembled and relocated into two less coherent units. This is not a *proof* of the correctness of the 2DH, but like a lawyer's narrative based on the evidence, it aims at providing a credible narrative that takes the data into account and does so in a more satisfactory manner than the opposing lawyer's narrative.

In fact, with the 2GH one has to assume that after Matthew 4:13 Luke *consistently* dislocated sayings from their Matthean contexts and reassembled them in ways that are rarely as coherent as the Matthean constructions. In the Sermon on the Mount alone Luke must have dislocated thirteen sayings instead of keeping them together in his Sermon on the Plain (6:20b–49). The sheer scale of Luke's dislocations and the inability of defenders of the 2GH to offer a coherent account of Luke's editorial procedures constitute a severe disadvantage to this hypothesis.

One might also ask: why would Luke omit such Matthaean passages as 6:1–4, which criticizes ostentatious displays of largesse, or 6:5–6, which concerns public displays of piety? With the 2GH Luke took over from Matthew the immediately preceding sayings (Matt. 5:43–48 = Luke 6:27–36) and the following saying (Matt. 6:9–13 = Luke 11:2–4). One cannot argue that Luke is not interested in almsgiving: he clearly is, as Luke 11:41 and 12:33 show. Nor can one argue that Luke is not critical of the kinds of behavior that advertise one's own honor, for Luke 14:7–11 is precisely an attack on self-aggrandizing behavior. Nor can one suggest that Luke is not interested in promoting a kind of prayer that does not draw attention to the agent, for Luke's story of the Pharisee and the toll collector (18:9–14) is precisely a story that contrasts ostentatious prayer with humble and self-effacing prayer. Given these clearly Lukan emphases, it becomes very difficult to imagine why Luke would have passed over Matthew 6:1–4, 5–6, as the 2GH requires.

Again it might be possible that with some ingenuity, an editorial scenario might be proposed to respond to these objections. None so far has been proposed, and so we are left with serious difficulties in rendering the Two Gospel hypothesis an *effective hypothesis*—one that offers plausible editorial scenarios for understanding the compositional practices of Mark and Luke.

Mark without Q

An important alternative to the 2DH combines Markan priority with Luke's direct dependence on Matthew. First proposed by two American scholars, James H. Ropes and Morton Enslin, and espoused by several British scholars, notably Michael Goulder and Mark Goodacre, this hypothesis combines the advantages of Markan priority with the simplicity of a solution that does not require a hypothetical document to account for the double tradition in Matthew and Luke (see fig. 6).

The MwQH accounts for the data described above (pp. 20–21) in the following manner. Matthew and Luke do not agree with each other against Mark in the sequence of the triple tradition, not because they could not do so—after all, Luke has direct

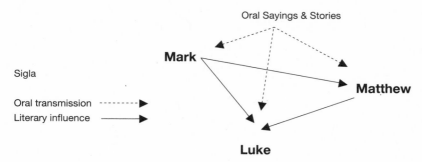

Figure 6. "Mark without Q" Hypothesis

contact with Matthew—but because *both* used Mark as a base text. Matthew had expanded Mark greatly, but nonetheless preserved some of Mark's wording. Although he rearranged what he found in Mark 1:29–6:12, after Mark 6:13 he agrees almost entirely with Markan sequence. So why did not Luke sometimes agree with Matthew's rearrangement of Mark? Goodacre conjectures that perhaps Luke had possessed a copy of Mark for up to "twenty years" prior to his discovery of Matthew, with the result that Mark's structure had already been fixed in Luke's mind.[16]

Goodacre invokes Luke's supposed prior knowledge of Mark to explain why Luke and Matthew disagree almost entirely on the relative placement of the double tradition (or Q) material. According to the MwQH, Luke must have disengaged every Q saying from the Markan setting that Matthew had given it and used it elsewhere. Goodacre argues that, since in most cases Luke had *already* used the Markan version as his primary source, he had to fit in Matthew's "Q" additions to Mark where best he could, which almost always meant relocating them.

For example, Matthew used the saying about having faith as a mustard seed (Matt. 17:20b) in a Markan context (Mark 9:14–29 || Matt. 17:14–21). Luke, who had also used the Markan pericope in Markan sequence (Luke 9:37–43), relocated the mustard seed saying to Luke 17:6. The phenomenon is observed again with Matthew's "twelve thrones" saying (19:28). Matthew added this saying to Mark's dialogue about the impossibility of the wealthy entering the kingdom (Matt. 19:23–30 || Mark 10:23–31). Luke had also used this Markan story (Luke 18:24–30). But when he saw that Matthew's version of the dialogue had an extra saying (Matt. 12:28), he moved it to 22:28–30.

It is in cases such as this that Goodacre's explanation begins to unravel. Did Luke have such reverence for Markan stories that he would not take over Matthew's additions? Goodacre must assume that in the two cases mentioned above Luke was so habituated to Mark's sequence *and to the content of Markan pericopae*, that he could not tolerate retaining these Matthean additions to Mark, even though both sayings are smoothly integrated into the Markan pericope by Matthew.

Is this a credible belief? It is difficult to imagine that Luke was so fixed in his use of Mark that he could not take over Matthew's modifications of Mark. After all, Luke was perfectly able to modify Mark's wording when it suited him. On MwQH it is not only these two sayings (Matt 17:20b; 19:28) that Luke dislocated from their Matthean contexts: he also moved Luke 13:28–29 (from Matt. 8:5–13), Luke 9:57–60 (from Matt. 8:18–27), Luke 10:13–15 (from Matt. 11:16–19), Luke 12:10 (from Matt. 12:31–37), Luke 13:18–20 (from Matt. 13:1–35), Luke 13:34–35 (from Matt. 23:1–39), Luke 14:16–24 (from Matt. 21:33–22:14), Luke 14:26–27 and 17:33 (from Matt. 10:7–42), Luke 15:4–7 and 17:3–4 (from Matt. 18:6–22), Luke 17:23–24, 37 (from Matt. 24:23–28), Luke 17:26–27, 34–35 (from Matt. 23:29–41), and Luke 19:12–26 (from Matt. 25:14–30). As with the 2GH, it is the sheer scale of dislocation and relocation that must be imagined that cumulatively makes the MwQH seem incredible. Surely it was *possible* for Luke to dismantle Matthaean pericopae, but *why* would he do it?

Luke in fact betrays no awareness of the particular ways that Matthew attached sayings to Mark's framework. Luke's woes against the Pharisees (11:37–54) are delivered in the house of an anonymous Pharisee who lived outside of Judea. Matthew's woes, delivered to a crowd, are attached to Mark's attack on the scribes (12:37b–40), posed out of doors in Jerusalem. Luke later took over Mark's attack on the scribes (12:37b–40 || Luke 20:45–47), the

very text that Matthew used for attaching his woes. Why would
Luke bother detaching Matthew's woes from their Markan setting? In the case of the Jerusalem word (13:34–35), Luke has also
avoided its Matthean setting in Jerusalem, placing it in some
nameless location in Samaria, in response to the comments of
some Pharisees (13:31–33). It might be tempting to think that the
presence of Pharisees in 13:31–33 is an echo of Matthew 23. But
in that case, Luke has completely reversed the characterization of
the Pharisees, who in 13:31–33 seem to be *friendly* to Jesus, not
hostile. For the MwQH Luke's procedure raises more questions
than it solves.

The phenomena discussed above in fact pose less difficulty for
the Two Document hypothesis, since one *ought* to expect Matthew
and Luke to combine Mark with Q differently. Moreover, we
should not expect Matthew's placement of Q pericopae to have
influenced Luke's choices, or vice versa, since Matthew and Luke
were working independently. Thus, if Matthew chose to combine
Q 17:5–6 (on having faith like a mustard seed) with Mark 9:28–30
to produce Matthew 17:19–22, there is no reason to expect that
Luke would have done the same; and in fact Luke used his two
sources, Mark and Q, quite differently. That is, contrary to the
MwQH, Luke behaves as if he had *not* seen Matthew's work, just
as the 2DH predicts.

As long as one cannot supply a plausible editorial scenario for
Luke's systematic disassembling Matthean units and relocating
Matthean sayings to other contexts, the MwQH cannot be
regarded as a good hypothesis.[17]

Complexities and Problems

Is the Two Document hypothesis without problems? Of course
not. Two possible sets of data pose difficulties for the 2DH:
"Mark-Q overlaps" and the so-called minor agreements.

Mark-Q Overlaps

As was pointed out above (p. 7), Matthew and Luke tend not to
agree against Mark's wording of a pericope and never agree

against Mark's sequence. There are some points where Matthew and Luke have a longer version of a saying or story than that preserved in Mark, and these the 2DH treats as Mark-Q overlaps—points where a story existed in both Mark and Q, and where Matthew or Luke or both have used both versions. Typically, the Q version is longer and has a larger sayings component. Apart from three Q pericopae concerning John the Baptist and the temptation that Matthew and Luke have connected with Mark in the same way (above, p. 17), Matthew and Luke always place the Mark-Q combination differently. For example, Mark and Q both had Jesus defending himself against the charge of exorcizing demons by Beelzebul and responding to a demand that Jesus produce a sign. In Mark the two were narrated separately, the Beelzebul accusation in Mark 3:22–27 and the request for a sign in Mark 8:11–12. In Q the two stories were joined. Matthew and Luke both chose to narrate the stories joined, as Q had them, but Matthew joined these to Mark 3:22–27, 28–30 and placed them just before the parables discourse (Mark 4:1–34 = Matt 13:1–35). Luke located the stories in his travel section (11:14–32), long after Mark's parable discourse (Mark 4:1–25 = Luke 8:4–18), after his teachings on prayer. Typically, Q's version of the request for a sign is longer than the corresponding Markan version.

Note here that not only do Matthew and Luke (and hence, Q) have the double saying about the Queen of the South and the Ninevites, which Matthew and Luke reproduce almost verbatim (*italics*); they also have a slightly different version of Jesus' answer. Neither absolutely refuses a sign, as Mark does; instead, both offer a cryptic sign: no sign *except the sign of Jonah*. Matthew and Luke then supply two different interpretations of this enigmatic sign of Jonah, but they do so using the same structure: "just as . . . so will the son of man . . . ," indicating that Q also had some interpretive saying. Note too that both Matthew and Luke have been influenced by some of Mark's wording (underscored). Matthew takes over the Pharisees as the interlocutors, and Luke takes over "testing him" and asking for a sign "from heaven" (i.e., from God). But Luke has not been influenced by what Matthew took from Mark ("the Pharisees") or what he added to Mark ("Teacher," "adulter-

Matthew 12:38–42	*Mark 8:11–12*	*Luke 11:16, 29–32*
[38]Then some of the scribes and <u>Pharisees</u> said to him, "Teacher, we wish to see a *sign* from you." [39]But he answered them, "An *evil* and adulterous *generation seeks for a sign; but no sign shall be given to it except the sign of Jonah* the prophet. [40]*For as Jonah* was three days and three nights in the belly of the whale, *so will the Son of man* be three days and three nights in the heart of the earth. [42]*The queen of the South will arise at the judgment with*	[11]The <u>Pharisees</u> came and began to argue with him, seeking from him a *sign* <u>from heaven, testing him.</u> [12]And he groaned in his spirit and said, "Why does this generation seek a sign? Truly, I say to you, no sign shall be given to this generation."	[16]while others, <u>testing him,</u> sought from him a *sign* <u>from heaven. . . .</u> [29]When the crowds were increasing, he began to say, 'This generation is an *evil generation*; it *seeks a sign, but no sign shall be given to it except the sign of Jonah.* [30]*For as Jonah* became a sign to the men of Nineveh, *so will the Son of man* be to this generation. [31]*The queen of the South will arise at the judgment with*
this generation and condemn it; *for she came from the ends of the earth to hear the wisdom of Solomon, and behold, something greater than Solomon is here.* [41]*The men of Nineveh will arise at the judgment with this generation and condemn it; for they repented at the preaching of Jonah, and behold, something greater than Jonah is here."*		the men of *this generation and condemn* them; *for she came from the ends of the earth to hear the wisdom of Solomon, and behold, something greater than Solomon is here.* [32]*The men of Nineveh will arise at the judgment with this generation and condemn it; for they repented at the preaching of Jonah, and behold, something greater than Jonah is here."*

ous," "the prophet"). For his part, Matthew is uninfluenced by Luke's rewording of Mark ("when the crowds were increasing"). This is just as one would expect if Matthew and Luke were editing Mark and Q independently of each other.

Although a few critics of the 2DH make much of the Mark-Q overlaps as a significant problem, these really pose little difficulty. In the first place, it is hardly surprising that two independent tellings of the Jesus tradition (Mark and Q) should sometimes narrate the *same* events or sayings. And they do:

> John's Preaching (Mark 1:2–6, 7–8 || Q 3:2, 7–9, 16–17)
> Jesus' Testing (Mark 1:12–13 || Q 4:1–13)
> The Beelzebul Accusation (Mark 3:22–27 || Q 11:14–26)
> The Request for a Sign (Mark 8:11–12 || Q 11:16, 29–32)
> Revelation of the Hidden (Mark 4:24 || Q 12:2–3, 4–7)
> The Parable of the Mustard Seed (and Yeast) (Mark 4:30–32 || Q 13:18–19, 20–21)
> The Mission Instruction (Mark 6:8–13 || Q 9:57–60; 10:2–16)
> Carrying One's Cross/Losing One's Life (Mark 8:34–35 || Q 14:26–27; 17:33)
> On Divorce (Mark 10:11–12 || Q 16:18)
> On False Messiahs (Mark 13:21–22 || Q 17:20–21, 23–37)

In the second place, in all of these overlaps, the Q version always gives attention to Jesus' (or John's) sayings and is longer (except in the divorce saying, which is about the same length as Mark's saying). And after Matthew 4:13 || Luke 4:16, Matthew and Luke *never* agree in using the Mark-Q overlaps in precisely the same way.

Thus Mark and Q were not entirely discontinuous accounts of Jesus. They overlapped sometimes, just as John's Gospel partially overlaps the Synoptics, or the *Gospel of Thomas* has some of the same sayings as those preserved in the Synoptics. The Mark-Q overlaps do not constitute a real problem for the Two Document hypothesis.

The Minor Agreements

If the Mark-Q overlaps could be called the major agreements of Matthew and Luke against Mark, there are also a number of smaller agreements of Matthew and Luke against Mark where there is no strong reason to suppose that there was another non-Markan version lurking behind Matthew and Luke. These kinds of agreements are not a problem for either the 2GH or the MwQH, since both posit a direct relationship between Matthew and Luke. It is only surprising that there are not more of them if Luke knew Matthew. For the 2DH, however, where Matthew and Luke edited Mark independently, such agreements should not be very plentiful, especially if they are not simply coincidental agreements.

Some of the minor agreements are not especially troublesome, since they concern the improvement of Mark's syntax. Both Matthew and Luke improved Mark's syntax by eliminating redundancies or particular Markan idiosyncrasies. Both replaced his excessive use of "and" with proper subordination and created more compact sentences. Sometimes they do so in the same way. But there are more problematic minor agreements, such as in the story of the woman with the hemorrhage.

Matt 9:20	*Mark 5:27*	*Luke 8:44*
[20] . . . <u>approaching</u> (*proselthousa*) *from behind,*	[27]. . . coming up (*elthousa*) *from behind* in the crowd	[44]<u>approaching</u> (*proselthousa*) *from behind,*
she touched <u>the fringe</u> of *his garment,*	*she touched* *his garment*	*she touched* *the fringe* of *his garment;*
[21]*for she was saying* to herself, "*If I* only *touch his garment I will be saved.*"	[28]*for she was saying,* "*If I touch* even *his garment I will be saved.*"	
		and immediately her flow of blood ceased.

That Matthew and Luke would choose to use the verb "to approach" (*proserchomai*) instead of "to come" (*erchomai*) is not a very significant agreement, since both evangelists often use compound verbs in place of Mark's simple verb "to come." Hence, sometimes they use the same compound. "To approach" is an especially common verb in Matthew, who uses it to signal the approach of someone with faith.

The more troublesome agreement is the common addition of "fringe," the tassels along the edge of Jesus' tunic or cloak. None of the explanations offered for this coincidence is particularly compelling. In Mark's scene there is a crush of people, and yet Jesus is able to discern that "power had gone out from him" because someone had touched him. He has to inquire who was responsible for this "discharge" of power, and the woman fearfully confesses (Mark 5:29–33). Matthew, however, has eliminated the crush of the crowd and so the dynamics of the scene change. He typically represents Jesus as responding to gestures of faith—men bringing a paralytic on a stretcher, a centurion coming to meet Jesus with a request. Matthew does not depict the woman's gesture as effecting the healing, as in Mark, but only as a sign of her faith. In the next verse Jesus then sees her faith and declares her healed, and only then is the woman healed. Matthew may have substituted "fringe" for the whole of Jesus' garment in order to stress the fact that Jesus was aware of even the most insignificant of touches, especially when that touch was a gesture of faith. But this is just a guess.

Although Luke also chose to highlight the fringe of Jesus' garment, it was likely for different reasons. In Acts 5:15 Luke says that the mere shadow of Peter healed people. Accordingly, if Luke treated the tassels of Jesus' garment like Peter's shadow, his point may have been that even the most insignificant parts of Jesus' person were still able to convey healing power.

Although Matthew and Luke seem to use the fringe differently, we are still left to explain why both picked this detail of Jesus' clothing to highlight. It might be that Mark's expression, "if I touch *even* his garment," suggested to both Matthew and Luke to stress the most insignificant part of that clothing. Matthew's addition might have been inspired by Mark himself, who in Mark 6:56 says, "And wherever he came, in villages, cities, or country, they laid the sick in the market places, and besought him that they might touch even the fringe [*kraspedon*] of his garment; and as many as touched it were made well." Some have suggested that Matthew might have in mind Zechariah 8:23, "Thus says the LORD of hosts: In those days ten men from the nations of every tongue shall take hold of the tassels [*kraspedon*] of a Jew, saying, "Let us go with you, for we have heard that God is with you." But it seems unlikely that both Matthew and Luke would have coincidentally had Zechariah 8:23 in mind.

We are left with no convincing editorial explanation of the common addition of "fringe." Is this fatal to the 2DH? Most adherents of the hypothesis do not think so, since the number of difficult minor agreements is quite small. In addition to the fringe in Mark 5:27, there are only three really problematic agreements: at Mark 4:11, Matthew and Luke have "to you it is given *to know* the *mysteries* of the kingdom of the heavens/God," while Mark has "to you the *mystery* of the kingdom of God is given"; at Mark 9:19 both Matthew and Luke add "and perverse" to Mark's "you faithless generation"; and at Mark 14:65, Matthew and Luke have "prophesy, who is it that struck you?" in place of Mark's "prophesy!" There is no good reason to suppose that there was a Q version of these sayings to account for the Matthew-Luke agreement, and editorial explanations are not terribly convincing.

It is not that we are without explanatory models to solve these problems, however. At least four kinds of explanations have been offered, all having some degree of plausibility. Some critics insist that coincidental editing by Matthew and Luke can still adequately explain all of the minor agreements, even these difficult ones (*redactional model*). Or it has been suggested that interference from oral tradition might account for some of the minor agreements. As most now admit, the transmission of Mark (and Q) was not a purely literary process. In a mostly illiterate culture, people knew the Jesus traditions because documents were performed orally by those who could read. That is, documents were *re-oralized*, with the document acting more like a musical script for performance than a text to be read. Such performances likely contained embellishments and explanations that could have found their way into later transcriptions by Matthew and Luke (*oral interference model*). Others have suggested that the minor agreements, taken together, all point to a *post-Markan* development. Thus, they argue that the copy of Mark which Matthew and Luke used (Mark II) was already a development beyond Mark's original Gospel (Mark I), copies of which we have (*deutero-Markus model*). Finally, it is common to note that the earliest manuscript of Mark that we have—the Chester Beatty I papyrus, known as $\mathfrak{P}^{45}$—is from two centuries after the composition of the Gospel, and our earliest manuscripts of Matthew and Luke date from almost a century after the composition of those Gospels. During the time between the composition of the Gospels and our earliest manuscripts, there are bound to have been alterations of the text. Hence, Matthew and Luke's minor agreements might either record what Mark originally wrote, but which was subsequently corrupted, or the Markan reading might have been the original Matthew-Luke reading, but in the meantime scribal transmission altered their texts or created agreements between Matthew and Luke that are not original (*scribal interference model*). We might represent these models pictorially as in figure 7.

Conclusion

In considering scholarly hypotheses about the relationship among the Gospels, we must keep in mind that they are hypotheses, not fact. They are also simplifications of the actual relationships among the Gospels. Our portraits of Synoptic relationships are just that: paintings that highlight some details, not photographs, and certainly not a full description of what happened.

We can never know exactly how the Gospels were related. Even if the Two Document hypothesis is a good approximation of Gospel relationships, it is unlikely that Matthew and Luke used the same copy of Mark or Q. At a minimum the copies of Mark used by Matthew and Luke were *different* copies, and likely different from the autograph of Mark, in at least small ways. Copyists typically introduced changes, deliberately or inadvertently.

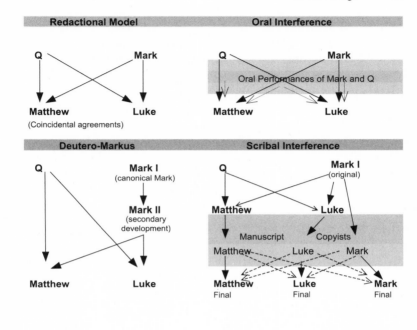

Figure 7. Models of Transmission of the Jesus Tradition

Since we do not have the autographs of *any* of the Gospels—our earliest manuscripts are all much later—we cannot be sure that the Greek texts of the Gospels that we use are identical with what the Synoptic evangelists wrote. We cannot even be sure that Matthew, or Mark, or Luke did not write multiple drafts of each of the Gospels. In other words, in spite of the seeming clarity that diagrams such as figure 3 imply, the real picture of Synoptic relationships was undoubtedly more complicated.

A good hypothesis does two things. First, it tries to make maximal sense of the available data. Good Synoptic hypotheses cannot provide compelling explanations of every bit of data, any more than hypotheses in the natural or social sciences can. Every hypothesis has to accommodate anomalous data—data that doesn't quite fit. A good hypothesis thus tries to be a good approximation, a schematic picture that fits most of the data, most of the time.

A good hypothesis does something else too: it provides an *effective* explanation—an explanation that aids our understanding of the data. To assume that Matthew and Luke used Mark independently, supplementing, improving, explaining, and qualifying Mark, in fact makes sense of most of the data of the Synoptic Gospels. *It works.* It produces an account of the Gospels that makes sense. To assume that Matthew and Luke used a second document to supplement what they had from Mark in fact makes for an efficient explanation of the data. *It works.*

Chapter Two

Reconstructing a Lost Gospel

If Matthew and Luke independently used Q, how do we know its contents? This is a question that has several layers. We might first ask about the general contents of Q—the kinds of sayings and stories it contained. Then we could ask whether what Matthew and Luke took from Q represents its full extent, or whether either or both evangelists might have omitted some of Q. Finally, we can ask about precise details of wording—does Matthew's rendition of Q better represent the original, or does Luke's? Or have both adapted the wording of Q so that its original wording is lost to our view?

Minimal Q

We can get a general idea of the contents of Q simply by isolating two sets of materials:

    (a) those sayings and stories preserved jointly by Matthew and Luke that are not in Mark, and

    (b) those sayings and stories where Matthew and Luke agree in having a substantially different version than that preserved by Mark (called Mark-Q overlaps).

The first set are sayings that Matthew and Luke *added* to Mark, although they usually did not combine Q with Mark in the same way. The second set are sayings and stories that Matthew and Luke either *conflated* with Markan versions of the story, or used *instead of* Mark's version.

The Beatitudes (Matt. 5:3–4, 6, 10–12 ‖ Luke 6:20–23) and John's preaching (Matt. 3:7–10 ‖ Luke 3:7–9) are examples of the first set of sayings. While Mark's Jesus is frequently depicted as teaching, Mark has relative few sayings of Jesus. Q offered to Matthew and Luke a rich source of John the Baptist's and Jesus' sayings with which they could dramatically expand Mark's Gospel. Thus, where Mark simply states that Jesus was teaching and preaching (Mark 1:22, 39—the point in Mark where Matthew inserts his Sermon on the Mount) and that large crowds followed Jesus (Mark 3:7–12—the point where Luke's Sermon on the Plain is added), Matthew and Luke could record Jesus' words: the Beatitudes and many other sayings. Likewise, Matthew and Luke inserted John's warnings to the crowds, taken from Q, into Mark 1:2–6, thereby dramatizing Mark's rather bare report that John came "preaching a baptism of repentance for the forgiveness of sins."

The second, smaller set of materials includes the temptation story (Matt. 4:1–11 ‖ Luke 4:1–13) and the parables of the Mustard Seed and the Yeast (Matt. 13:31–33 ‖ Luke 13:18–21) and the other Mark-Q overlaps listed above (p. 34). Q's temptation story, reflected in Matthew and Luke, is an elaborate three-part debate between Jesus and the devil, while the Markan version (1:12–13) is a brief two-verse story with no speech at all. Since it would make no sense to have Jesus tested twice, Matthew and Luke *conflated* the Markan and the Q stories and thus produced accounts with both Markan and Q elements. At other points where Mark overlapped Q, Matthew and Luke might opt for one account over the other. All three Gospels have the parable of the Mustard Seed, but Matthew and Luke agree *against Mark* in enough details to make one think that they had access to a second (Q) version of the parable. This suspicion is confirmed by the fact that both immediately add another parable that is lacking in Mark entirely, the parable of the Yeast. Matthew conflated Q's double parable (Mustard + Yeast) with Mark's parable of the Mustard Seed (4:30–32). Luke, however, passed over Mark's Mustard Seed when he copied Mark's parable discourse (Mark 4:1–34, cf. Luke 8:4–18) and placed Q's double parable after the healing of a crippled woman (Luke 13:10–17). Luke apparently preferred Q's version to Mark's.

If we combine all the materials in (a) and (b) above, we arrive at the following set of Q texts (I will refer to Q texts by their *Lukan* versification; Mark-Q overlaps are in italic):

John's preaching (3:7b–9, *16b*–17)
the temptation (*4:1–13*)
Jesus' first speech (6:20b–23, 27–33, 35, 36–*38*, 39–49)
the centurion's serving boy (7:1–2, 6–10)
John's question (7:18–19, 22–23)
Jesus' words about John (7:24–28, 31–35)
two volunteers (9:57–60)
Jesus' mission instructions and thanksgiving (10:2–3, *4–11*, 12–16, 21–22, 23b–24)
instructions on prayer (11:2–4, 9–13)
the Beelzebul accusation and request for a sign (11:*14–18*, 19–20, *21–22*, 23, 24–26, *29–30*, 31–32, 33–35)
woes against the Pharisees and scribes (11:39–44, 46–52)

two parables (13:*18–19*, 20–21)
the Two Ways (13:24, 26–27, 28–30)
a lament over Jerusalem (13:34–35)
"exalting the humble" (14:11/18:14)
the parable of the Great Supper and sayings about following Jesus (14:16–24, 26-27; *17:33*)
insipid salt (*14:34–35*)
the parable of the Lost Sheep (15:4–7)
"God or mammon" (16:13)
sayings on the Torah (16:16, 17, *18*)
sayings on scandals, forgiveness, and faith (17:*1b*–2, 3b–4, *6b*)
the coming of the Son of Man (17:*23–24*, 26–27, 30, 34–35, 37b)

admonitions on anxiety (12:2–8,
    9–12, 22b–31, 33–34)
the coming Son of Man
    (12:39–40, 42b–46, 51–53,
    54b–56, 58–59)

the parable of the Entrusted
    Money (19:12–13,
    15b–26)
sitting on thrones (22:28–30)

When in 1988 I surveyed two dozen previous reconstructions of Q ranging from the late nineteenth century to the 1980s, there was very little disagreement among scholars on the basic contents of Q or what we might call "minimal Q."[1]

Of course some questions may still be raised. Is it possible, for example, that some of the sayings jointly preserved by Matthew and Luke did not come from Q, but from some other oral or written source? That is indeed a possibility, and just this possibility has been proposed by a few scholars in respect of the parable of the Great Supper, where the verbal agreement between Matthew and Luke is very low, or in the case of a floating maxim such as "many of the last will be first, and the first will be last" (Q 13:30). One can imagine such floating sayings to have found their way into Matthew and Luke quite independently of written sources, or Matthew and Luke might coincidentally have included a parable that was not taken from Mark or Q but which had the same general narrative structure, as is the case with Matthew's Wedding Banquet (Matt. 22:1–10) and Luke's Great Supper (Luke 14:16–24). It is much more difficult to appeal to this kind of explanation, however, when the verbal agreement between Matthew and Luke is high, and when Matthew and Luke also agree in placing Q texts in the same relative sequence, as they do about one-half of the time. Moreover, low verbal agreement between Matthew and Luke is not ultimately a good reason to exclude double tradition sayings from Q, as I shall explain later (p. 56).

Even if we were to exclude a few sayings from Q, what remains displays a remarkable degree of literary and thematic coherence, as Arland Jacobson has shown.[2] Q has forms of sayings that are otherwise uncommon in Mark (makarisms, woes, correlatives, and prophetic threats). The forms that Q shares with Mark (miracle stories, parables) are used in a noticeably different manner than in Mark. In addition, as I shall indicate in chapter 3, Q contains elements that lend the collection an overarching unity.

Expanding Minimal Q?

A frequent question is whether Matthew and Luke might have omitted some of Q. In that case, of course, some of Q would be forever lost, unless we were to discover some other document that preserved Q or a copy of Q itself. Since both Matthew and Luke omitted a few Markan pericopae entirely (Mark 3:20–21; 4:26–29; 8:22–26; 14:51–52) and some parts of Markan pericopae, it is possible that both also omitted some of Q. Eric Eve has proposed a thought experiment in which he tried to reconstruct "Mark" from Matthew and Luke, supposing that we have the text of Q, not Mark.[3] Eve found that this reconstructed Mark had very little that it should not contain and that Mark's sequence of pericope could be reconstructed correctly. It would, however, be shorter than our Mark, due mainly to the Mark-Q overlaps, which tend to favor Q's wording and obscure Mark's, and to Luke's "great omission" of Mark 6:45–8:22.

While it is possible that Matthew and Luke jointly omitted some of Q, there is reason to think that they did not omit much. Together, Matthew and Luke preserve all but 31 of Mark's 666 verses,[4] and Matthew has all but 55 (92 percent) of Mark's verses. This suggests that together Matthew and Luke were quite conservative with their sources. Moreover, a close comparison of Matthew and Luke indicates that they tend to preserve the wording of Q *better* on average than the wording of Mark.[5] This is not simply because Q is predominantly sayings of Jesus, which we should expect to be preserved more faithfully; in fact Matthew and Luke also preserve the narrative bits of Q better than they preserve the narrative portions of Mark. Of course we cannot be sure that some of Q was not omitted, but the general tendencies of Matthew and Luke suggest that they preserved a very large proportion of the document.

Special Material

A more complicated question concerns the possibility that either Matthew or Luke omitted a unit from Q and the other evangelist preserved it. Both evangelists, after all, omitted parts of Mark. Matthew does not have Mark 1:23–28; 1:35–38; 11:18–19; and 12:41–44, while Luke omitted Mark 4:33–34 and all of Mark 6:45–8:26. If they did the same with Q, this would mean that some of the material that appears only in Matthew and only in Luke in fact came from Q. This material, called "special material," includes such sayings as Luke's woes (6:24–26), which are the mirror image of Q's beatitudes, or Matthew 5:41, on going an extra mile, which is found in the midst of other sayings from Q, or Luke's parable of the Lost Drachma, found attached to the Q parable of the Lost Sheep.

Scholars differ in their approaches to special material. On one end of the spectrum, a few include a good deal of special material, supposing that both Matthew and Luke omitted a good bit of Q. Others are minimalists, either assuming that Matthew and Luke did not omit much of Q, or holding that a reconstruction of Q should not include any material that is at all doubtful. I believe that a middle course should be steered, and that we can include a modest amount of special material, but only when stringent criteria are met. Sayings that appear in only Matthew or only Luke could be included in Q (1) when the saying in question is a component of texts already assigned to Q; (2) when it accords stylistically with other Q texts; (3) where there is no reason to suspect that Matthew or Luke has created the saying; (4) and when good reasons can be adduced why the other evangelist omitted it.[6]

Application of these principles results in only a slight expansion of Q. The International Q Project reconstruction includes only Matthew 5:41 (on going an extra mile), Luke 11:27–28 (a woman flattering Jesus in the crowd), Luke 15:8–10 (the Lost Drachma), Luke 17:20–21 (the kingdom of God is within you), and Luke 17:28–29 (the days of Lot).[7] I have argued for a few more sayings: Q/Matt. 11:23b–24 (Matthew's longer woe against Capernaum) and Luke 6:24–26 (Luke's woes), 9:61–62 (on putting one's hand to the plough), and 12:13–14, 16–21 (on inheritance and wealth).[8]

Let me illustrate the kind of arguments that go into including a piece of special material in Q. The parable of the Lost Drachma occurs only in Luke (15:8–10) but should be assigned to Q.

First, in Luke this parable forms a pair with the Q parable of the Lost Sheep (Luke 15:4–7 || Matt. 18:12–14). Thus, it is found in a Q context. Second, from a stylistic point of view it strongly resembles both the parable of the Lost Sheep and other Q texts. Both the Lost Sheep and the Lost Drachma take the form, "what man/woman among you, having *x* and if he or she loses it . . . will not seek until he or she finds it. . . . And rejoicing . . ." The opening formula is also found in other Q parables such as Q 11:11 ("what father among you . . .") and Q 12:25 ("who among you . . ."). Moreover, the double parable of a man with sheep and a woman with the drachmas is an example of the phenomenon of *gender pairing*, found elsewhere in Q. Double illustrations, featuring a man's activity and a woman's, appear frequently in Q: Q 11:31–32 (the Queen of the South and Jonah); 12:24–28 (those who farm; those who spin); 13:18–21 (a man sowing and a woman making bread); and 17:34–35 (two men in a field; two women at a grindstone).

Third, although a few scholars think that Luke inserted the parable of the Lost Drachma from some other source, this suggestion is highly unlikely. It is highly unlikely that Q and some completely independent source would contain two parables that were almost identical in form. The only viable alternatives are that the parable is from Q or that it is a Lukan creation, modeled on Q 15:4–7. But no one has been able to suggest a reason for Luke creating the second parable. Luke has three parables in chapter 15—the Lost Sheep, the Lost Drachma, and the Lost Son—each featuring a celebration and the proclamation that "what was lost has been found" (15:6, 9, 24, 32). These motifs constitute an editorial refrain that answers the Pharisees' complaint about Jesus' dining with sinners (Luke 15:1–3). The most dramatic of these parables is the third, featuring a human who sins and returns; the *least* effective is the Lost Drachma, an inanimate object, which can neither sin nor repent. Thus, it is unlikely that Luke composed the Lost Drachma, since it does not effectively illustrate his theme. But in view of Q's penchant for paired male-female illustrations, the case is strong for derivation from Q. Stronger, in fact, for without Luke's emphasis on repentance and his apologetic for Jesus' dining habits, the economics of the two parables comes into sharper focus: it is a poor shepherd who has a small flock of one hundred sheep and must care for them himself; it is a poor woman who has a life savings of only ten drachmas, less than one month's wage. Both are quite unlike a man in the next parable, with his servants, robes, shoes, rings, and fatted calves. In other words, the first two parables cohere with the village or small-town environment otherwise thought to reflect the situation of Q.

Finally, we must ask why Matthew would omit the parable of the Lost Drachma. The reason is plain. Matthew used the parable of the Lost Sheep—something that could wander off and return—as part of his extended exhortation in chapter 18 to seek those who had sinned. The parable of the Lost Drachma would simply not fit: it is an inanimate object that could not wander off.

The evidence favors Luke 15:8–10 being derived from Q. The parable is found in a Q context and it is stylistically consistent with Q; indeed it displays Q's characteristic use of gender-paired illustrations. It is unlikely that Luke created the illustration, since his main point comes not in the parable of the Lost Drachma, but in the parable of the Prodigal Son. On the other hand, Matthew cannot have preserved the parable in the context in which he used the Lost Sheep. These arguments, taken together, constitute a good case for the inclusion of Luke 15:8–10 in Q.

Some Problematic Passages

As I argued above, pericopae called Mark-Q overlaps, where Matthew and Luke agree in having a *substantially* different version than that preserved by Mark, can be assigned to Q. But what is a "substantial" disagreement with Mark?

The account of Jesus' baptism illustrates the problem. It is found in all three Gospels. Ordinarily, then, we would suppose that Matthew and Luke took their account from Mark. There are, however, a few respects in which Matthew and Luke agree *against* Mark, agreements that may signal the presence of a Q version of the baptism.[9] Some scholars have added that Q in fact *requires* an account in which Jesus was acclaimed as Son of God if the devil's challenge in Q 4:1–13, "if you are the Son of God," is to make sense. But these arguments have failed to persuade others, who point out that each of the minor agreements between Matthew and Luke is entirely explicable on the basis of Matthean and Lukan editorial habits. Thus, the agreements of Matthew and Luke are simply coincidental. Moreover, the argument that Q requires a narrative which identified Jesus as the Son of God is flawed: none of the Gospels offer accounts that explain the titles "son of Man," "Christ," or "Son," and yet they use these titles without hesitation. Since Synoptic experts are nearly evenly divided on whether to include the baptism of Jesus in Q, I think it best to exclude it.[10]

Matthew 3:2–6 ‖ Luke 3:2–4 offer another complex case. Again there is a Markan parallel (1:2–6), and Matthew and Luke display a relatively high degree of verbal agreement with Mark. Most of the agreements between Matthew and Luke—"John," "preaching," "in the wilderness," and the quotation of Isaiah 40:3—are based on Mark. Nevertheless, Matthew and Luke concur against Mark in the use of a rather unusual phrase, locating the story in "all the circuit of the Jordan" (*pasa he perichoros tou Iordanou*). This agreement might be taken as coincidental or trivial were it not for the fact that in the Hebrew Bible this phrase has a technical meaning, referring to the southern Jordan rift valley. The phrase appears almost exclusively in connection with the story of Lot and the destruction of Sodom (Gen. 13:10–12; 19:17, 25, 28). It seems unlikely that Matthew and Luke could have coincidentally added the phrase, for neither uses the phrase in its technical sense: Matthew confuses the area with the "wilderness of Judea" (Matt. 3:1), which does not include the rift valley, and Luke displays no specific knowledge of Judean geography at all. Moreover, the Lot story, with which the phrase is associated, does not play a special role in Matthew's or Luke's interpretation of John's ministry, for both, under Mark's influence, immediately associate John with the motif of restoration and repentance taken from Isaiah 40, not Genesis 19.

An allusion to the Lot story, however, coheres extremely well with what follows in Q. John's preaching refers to "*fleeing* from the wrath to come," appeals to a *kinship* with Abraham—Lot was Abraham's nephew—and to destructive fire and the transformation of "stones into kin of Abraham" (contrast the fate of Lot's wife). Q, moreover, has several other references and allusions to the Lot story (Q 10:12; Q/Matt. 11:23b–24; Q 17:28–29, 34–35), allusions that neither Matthew nor Luke developed.[11] Of course, Q cannot have simply begun, "You brood of vipers"; some introduction is necessary, and John must have been explicitly named. This means at the very least that John must have been named as the first speaker in Q and, given the vituperative tone of the speech, there must have been some indication of audience and setting. Recollection of the Lot story would fit this role admirably. For these reasons, the International Q Project has included portions of Luke 3:2b–3 in Q, albeit in a highly lacunal form: "John . . . all the circuit of the Jordan . . ."

On the basis of the foregoing, we can propose tentatively a reconstruction of Q. I place in double brackets ([[ ]]) sayings where there is considerable uncertainty, and in angle brackets (< >) pericopae that are not included in the International Q Project reconstruction but which this writer believes may also come from Q. Brace brackets ({ }) and smaller font are used for pericopae sometimes proposed for Q membership but which I do not think qualify (as always, Q texts are cited by their *Lukan* versification):

3:2b–3, 7–9, 16b–17 {21–22}; 4:1–13, 16; 6:20b–21, 22–23, <24–26>, 27–33, Q/Matt. 5:41, 34–35b, 35c, 36–37b, 38c, 39–45, 46–49; 7:1b, 3, 6b–10, 18–19, 22–23, 24–28, [[29–30]], 31–35; 9:57–60 <61–62>; 10:2–12, 13–15 <Q/Matt. 11:23b–24>, 16, {Q/Matt. 10:5b–6, 23} 21–22, 23–24 {25–28}; 11:2–4, {5–8}, 9–13, 14–20, [[21–22]], 23, 24–26, [[27–28]], 29–32, 33–35, 39–44, 46–52; 12:2–12, <13–14, 16–21>, 22–31, 33–34, {35–38}, 39–40, 42b–46, [[49]], 51–53,

54–56, 58–59; **13:**18–19, 20–21, 24, 26–27, 28–29, [[30]], 34–35; **14:**{5}, [[14:11]]; 14:16–24, 26–27; **17:**33; **14:**34–35; **15:**4–7, 8–10; **16:**13, 16, 17, 18; **17:**1b–2, 3b–4, 6b, {7–10}, [[20–21]], 23–24, 26–27, [[28–29]], 30, 34–35, 37b; **19:**12–13, 15b–26; **22:**28–30.

This does *not* represent a major expansion beyond "minimal Q": the inclusion of a few pieces of special material justified by rigorous argument would amount to a modest expansion of Q from 235 to 266 verses—only 31 additional verses. (See the appendix for an English text of Q, which represents this modest expansion of Q.)

The Wording of Q

If we can arrive at a picture of the general contents of Q, can we get a clearer idea of its wording? For about one-half of Q, the wording is already clear, since Matthew and Luke agree verbatim on slightly more than 50 percent of their Q words.[12] But there are, of course, disagreements. Can we decide which evangelist better preserved Q? Let me illustrate the process with a modern example.

Imagine taking two different newspapers, both of which ran a story taken from the Associated Press wire service. If you line up the stories side by side, it is obvious that the basic structure and much of the wording of the two stories have been taken verbatim from the AP story. There may be some differences in wording and emphasis. There may be differences in length. But if you know enough about the editorial policies of the two newspapers and their readerships, you could make educated guesses as to which editor had intervened in the story, which editor had shortened (or lengthened) it, and which editor had made changes and why.

A century of analysis of the Gospels has given scholars a good idea of the characteristic emphases and Greek style of each of the Synoptic writers. Matthew has a strong tendency to regard the activities of Jesus as fulfillment of texts of the Hebrew Bible and to have Jesus quote the Hebrew Bible. He also likes the connective "then" (*tote*) and the phrase "kingdom of the heavens," and to introduce

speech with phrases such as "and approaching (*proselthon*) *x* said."
Mark famously punctuates healings and exorcisms with a command
to keep silent, but also has a strong tendency to use "and" (*kai*) to
join clauses and to overuse the word "immediately" (*euthys*). Luke
stresses Jesus' piety and prayerfulness, and favors compound verbs
where Matthew and Mark have simple verbs.[13]

Let me take a famous difference in wording between Matthew
and Luke. In the first beatitude of Matthew's Sermon on the Mount
and Luke's Sermon on the Plain (which comes from Q), Matthew
has "Blessed are the *poor in spirit*, for theirs is the kingdom *of the
heavens*," while Luke has "Blessed are *the poor*, for yours is the kingdom *of God*." Of all the Gospel writers, only Matthew uses the
phrase "kingdom of the heavens." This does not automatically
mean that Luke's phrase is original. But when we observe that
where Mark has "kingdom of God," Matthew normally changed
this to "kingdom of the heavens" and that Luke retained Mark's
phrase, it becomes more likely that Q also had "kingdom of God"
and that "kingdom of the heavens" is Matthew's editorializing.

What of the other differences between Matthew's "poor in
spirit" and Luke's "poor"? "Poor in spirit" is another way of saying "humble." Thus the difference between Matthew's version
and Luke's is that Matthew is speaking about *moral characteristics*
and Luke about *social and economic states*. Which represents Q?
The clue comes from the fact that Matthew has more beatitudes
(nine) than Luke (four), and that all five of Matthew's extra beatitudes concern moral characteristics: meekness, showing mercy,
purity of heart, being a peacemaker, and willingness to be perse-
cuted for the sake of justice. In the second beatitude, where Luke
has "blessed are those who are hungry," Matthew has a moralized
version: "blessed are those who hunger and thirst *after justice*."
When we note the consistent way in which Matthew has moralized the beatitudes and added five extra moralizing beatitudes, it
is reasonable to conclude that Matthew's "poor in spirit" is editorial. Luke is not uninterested in morality, as an examination of
other parts of his Gospel shows. On the contrary, Luke is especially interested in depicting Jesus as merciful and seeking justice.
So it is quite unlikely that he would have deleted the moralizing

beatitudes had he seen them. The most probable conclusion, then, is that the original Q beatitude is "Blessed are you poor, for yours is the kingdom of God"; Luke took this over more or less unchanged, and Matthew moralized and supplemented it with additional beatitudes.

For more than a century and a half scholars have compared Matthew and Luke to determine the wording of Q by the kind of process that I have just outlined: identifying where the two already agree, and in the cases of disagreements deciding which evangelist altered the wording of Q by examining their editorial tendencies in general. This involves poring over hundreds of points of disagreements and deciding each case. Starting in 1985 a group of scholars began producing a collaborative reconstruction of Q which collected the past 160 years of scholarship on Q, and deciding each "variant" through an extended process of exhaustive data collection, debate, and editorial decision. The text of Q published by the International Q Project (IQP) in 2000 offers a reconstructed Q of about 4,500 words or about 260 verses, accompanied by a full database containing all previous reconstructions and arguments made in regard to the reconstruction of Q since 1838.[14]

How certain can we be about the wording and the contents of Q? What of the possibility that both Matthew and Luke decided to alter the text of Q? The answer is, it depends. In some cases we may have a high degree of certainty about some aspects of Q; in other cases, we are dealing only with general probabilities.

The International Q project borrowed a grading system from the United Bible Societies Greek New Testament for ranking its decisions in *Documenta Q* database. When Matthew and Luke are in agreement, the text of Q seems certain, except in a very few cases where the agreement seems to be coincidental. When strong reasons can be supplied for concluding, for example, that Matthew's version is editorial, and when there is no reason at all to suppose that Luke has tampered with his version, and when the Lukan version is completely consistent with Q style attested elsewhere, that reading is given an {A} or {B} ranking. In the *Critical Edition* and the English text of Q printed in the appendix of this book, these readings are printed in normal Roman font.

There are occasions, however, when either there are no strong reasons for doubting either Matthew or Luke, or where there are strong reasons for thinking that both are editorial. In these cases *Documenta Q* assigns a {C} or a {D} ranking, and the *Critical Edition* and English translations print the text in double square brackets ([[ ]]). When there is a great deal of doubt about a correct reconstruction, *Documenta Q* ranks the readings as {D}. In the *Critical Edition* these texts are signalled by the presence of question marks (?) enclosing the verse number. In the English text I have enclosed the translation in double angle brackets (« »), to provide a general sense of what may have been in Q, even though this is not a proper reconstruction. There are also points where Matthew and Luke appear to have edited Q so completely that nothing is left of the original, but Q must have had something. We cannot guess what it had. To summarize:

> Ordinary font: Portions of Q where either Matthew and Luke are in absolute agreement, or where strong arguments exist for deciding that either Matthew or Luke represents Q.
>
> [[Jesus]]: Double brackets indicate where there is considerable uncertainty about a reconstruction: there are either good arguments for suspecting both Matthew's version and Luke's as editorial, or no particularly strong arguments to support either. The IQP prints the version that has a slightly better probability of representing Q.
>
> «at that time»: Double angle brackets are used where the gist of the text is clear enough but its precise wording is not.
>
> . . . : Ellipses indicate where it is impossible to reconstruct Q at all.
>
> < > Angle brackets are used to signal an emendation in the text.

For example, it is clear that Q's beatitudes began with a blessing on the poor (Q 6:20b). The beatitudes appear to have been spoken to "disciples," but it is not completely clear whether Matthew's "opening his mouth" or Luke's "raising his eyes" was in the introductory phrase. The IQP inclined toward Luke here, and thus prints "and [[rais]]ing his [[eyes to]] his disciples he said" (Q 6:20a). In the temptation story, both Matthew and Luke indicate that Jesus was fasting but use different words to convey this. Because it is impossible to decide between Matthew and Luke, but it is clear that *both* conveyed the idea that Jesus was not eating, the IQP prints "«he ate nothing» for forty days" for Q 4:2. There also must have been an initial transitional phrase between the temptation story (Q 4:1–13) and the beginning of Q's sermon. But the wording of this transitional phrase is unknown, because both Matthew and Luke have created their own editorial transitions. Hence, the IQP prints . . . at the beginning of Q 6:20: something was likely there in Q, but we cannot reconstruct it or even guess what it was.

Oral or Written?

For much of the twentieth century Q was simply assumed to be a written document. This is perhaps because scholars who studied the Gospels and Q were themselves print-oriented and thought of early Christianity as a predominantly text-oriented movement. More recent scholarship has emphasized the fact that literacy rates in the ancient Mediterranean, including Jewish Palestine, were very low—between 3 and 10 percent.[15] Scholars have also stressed that this was an *oral-aural-scribal culture* where most communication was based not on reading but on hearing. A small class of literate persons, the scribes, served to prepare written communication when needed.

This fact does not necessarily require us to suppose that Q was oral. On the contrary, we know that there were many documents in antiquity, and the small scribal class was responsible for the production of everything from economic and legal documents to literary texts. What it does imply, however, is that the majority of the population could access written texts only through their *oral performance or recitation*. Thus, whether Q was a written text, as most scholars believe it to have been, or a set of oral traditions, most of the Jesus people knew the contents of Q through its public or private recitation.

Why would most scholars suppose that the material common to Matthew and Luke was written and not oral? The simple reason is that there are enough points where Matthew and Luke, in reproducing Q, are so strongly in agreement that we must suppose that they were looking at a written document. In fact only eight of Q's ninety-two pericopae display less than 20 percent agreement, and more than one-third display between 60 and 98 percent agreement.[16] This level of verbatim agreement is very difficult to explain *except* on the thesis that Matthew and Luke were copying a document. When you consider the fact that Matthew and Luke often relate multiple Q units *in the same relative sequence*, as was explained in the previous chapter, the conclusion is almost inescapable that they are using a written text. Even those scholars who believe that some of Q might really have been bits of oral tradition concede this point.[17]

As I have indicated above, there are also Q passages where Matthew and Luke have a very low degree of agreement, sayings such as the parables of the Great Supper (14:16–24: 15 percent), the Entrusted Money (19:12–27: 22 percent), and the admonition on forgiveness (17:4: 6 percent). Should we exclude these from Q and ascribe them to bits of oral tradition that have independently found their way into Matthew and Luke?

What makes our decision difficult is the fact that ancient editors could be very inconsistent in their use of sources. We might think that Matthew would have been consistent in how much he was prepared to paraphrase his sources and how much he would use verbatim. But this would be a mistake. We have examples where we know both the source used by an author and that author's work and can therefore examine how consistently they copied. Analysis shows that one author might use the *same* source text in a highly inconsistent fashion, sometimes copying most of its words, and at other times paraphrasing completely.[18] Hence, when we observe Matthew or Luke sometimes copying Q nearly exactly, and at other times departing from Q's wording (or at least disagreeing with the other evangelist's rendition), they were only acting as other ancient writers did, exercising freedom at some points and copying exactly at other points. Additionally, we know of authors such as Josephus who regularly paraphrased his sources almost completely, with the result that there is virtually no verbatim agreement between his sources (the Greek version of the Bible) and his text. Yet this is not a reason to doubt that he used the Bible. Such cases imply that it is *not* a legitimate inference that low-agreement pericopae such as the parable of the Great Supper or the Entrusted Money cannot be ascribed to the written text of Q, but must come from oral tradition.

Having said this, it is important to return to an earlier point and stress that despite the fact that Q was a document that Matthew and Luke used alongside another document (Mark), for most of the Jesus people Q was an *oral text*, performed in various settings. I shall return to this point in the final chapter when discussing what happened to Q.

The First Greek Gospel

Virtually all of the early documents of the Jesus movement, whether from Palestine, Syria, Asia Minor, Egypt, or Greece, were penned in Greek. This in spite of the fact that the earliest Jesus followers were likely Aramaic speakers. What about Q?

In the nineteenth and early part of the twentieth centuries, some scholars believed that Q was originally written in Aramaic and only subsequently translated into Greek. This belief can be traced in part to a statement by the early Christian writer Papias, who declared that "Matthew arranged the *logia* in the Hebrew language, and everyone interpreted [or: translated] them as he was able" (Eusebius, *Ecclesiastical History* 3.39.16). Some scholars, aware that Matthew's Gospel was not written in Aramaic but in Greek, concluded that Papias must have been referring to one of Matthew's sources, Q. Other scholars thought that they could detect in Matthew and Luke "translation variants"—points where the disagreement between Matthew and Luke's rendition of Q might be traced to alternate translations of the same Aramaic word.

As a comprehensive explanation this does not work. In the first place there are many points where Matthew and Luke agree verbatim in rendering Q, which means that they must have been

consulting a *Greek document*. The agreement is simply too high to
believe that the two translated Aramaic words of Jesus and coincidentally came up with exactly the same Greek translation. Anyone who is familiar with multiple languages will know that two
independent translators will seldom arrive at precisely the same
translation.

Advocates of translation hypotheses usually fix upon a handful
of individual words that might go back to differing translations of
an Aramaic word. For example, in the Lord's Prayer Matthew has
opheilema (debt; 6:12), where Luke has *hamartia* (sin; 11:4). Does
this go back to the Aramaic *ḥoba* (debt, sin) and imply that the two
must have rendered an Aramaic document? The answer, clearly,
is no. As Luke 13:2–4 and 7:41–50 make plain, Luke knows very
well that "debt" can be used as a metaphor for "sin." That he
chooses "sin" in the Lord's Prayer probably only means that Luke
is *also* aware that in Koine Greek *opheilema* normally refers to
monetary debts, not moral failings. Thus he avoids a misunder-
standing of the petition by substituting "sins." This substitution
allows him to preserve the cognate *opheilonti* in the second part of
the petition: "as we ourselves forgive everyone who is *indebted* to
us." That is, once Luke has made clear that the context is about
sin, he can preserve the second instance of *opheilo* and its implica-
tion that "sin" is a kind of "debt" owed to God or to others. What
would have been obvious to a Palestinian reader of Q needed to
be explained to Luke's reader in Greece or Asia Minor. We do not
need to appeal to a lost Aramaic original of Q in order to account
for the disagreement between Matthew and Luke.

Let me be clear on the point. The issue is not whether Q contains Aramaisms—it does, as various scholars have ably demonstrated. The issue is not whether Q was formulated in an
environment in which Aramaic speech patterns could influence its
language. The issue is whether Q was *written* in Aramaic. For this
supposition there is no compelling evidence. Although there are
some Aramaisms in Q, the density of Semitic syntax is not sufficiently high to indicate translation into Greek—that is, the kind of
Greek which results from a translator who allows the syntax of the
original language to influence the translation. Moreover, Q con-

tains a number of syntactical devices that are only possible in Greek, not Aramaic.[19] All of the evidence points to composition in Greek.

This conclusion might seem to create a puzzle. Why would Jesus' followers in Jewish Palestine (and probably the Galilee, as most recent critics think[20]) write their document in Greek? We cannot know with certainty, but one possible explanation is that the language of the scribes who composed Q was Greek, as it was overwhelmingly the scribal language in the Eastern Mediterranean. We have many hundreds of documents from Ptolemaic and Roman Egypt written on behalf of native Egyptians whose language was Demotic. But their documents—loans, leases, letters, oaths, club records, and so on—are written in Greek because this was the administrative language. We might think of the situation of India under British rule, where dozens of local languages were spoken, but the language of documents—the administrative language—was English. Accordingly, we might suppose that although the Jesus followers who collected and used the materials in Q spoke Aramaic as a first language, it was Greek that was used when their scribes set down Q in writing.

Who Wrote Q?

Who wrote Q? The answer might seem obvious: it must have been a scribe who was able to write. There were, however, many different levels of scribes, from those connected with the royal courts and the temple, to those associated with regional and city administration, to the village scribes—*komogrammateis*, official scribes associated with tax collection and administration at the local level—to various literate and semiliterate individuals who made a living by assisting others in preparing letters, petitions, leases, and other documents.

Scribal conventions have left their mark on Q. In the first place, the formative parts of Q—Q 6:20b–49; 10:2–11, 16; 11:2–4, 9–13; 12:2–8, 11–12; 12:22b–31—display the characteristics of an instruction, a well-known scribal genre attested in Proverbs 1–9, portions of Sirach, and in many examples of Egyptian scribal wisdom.[21] Among the repertoire of interests for Q are debt, the requisitioning of persons or animals, and divorce, all matters that concerned scribes in their daily activities. As Alan Kirk has observed, even the structure of Q's Lord's Prayer reflects the form of the administrative petition, which scribes composed on behalf of the illiterate as a regular part of their activities. It begins with a salutation and quickly moves to petitions. The petition section often deals with requests for debt relief, redress of wrongs, or matters pertaining to subsistence, the very topics of the Lord's Prayer. The petition sometimes concludes with references to the benevolence of the ruler.[22] Scribes composing Q naturally employed the scribal forms of discourse with which they were familiar.

Kirk's point apropos of Q is that Q should not be conceived of as a direct transcript of oral performances of Jesus tradition. On the contrary, Q already displays the signs that its various speeches have been standardized in their form, no longer displaying the idiosyncratic characteristics of oral performance. Rather than being the records of oral performances, Q's speeches are

> *scripts for performance* . . . operative at the highly charged oral-written interface, and hence not fixed in the absolute sense but in their written transmission open to various sorts of transmission.[23]

Q as a "Gospel"

A final note. It is now common to call Q "the Sayings Gospel Q" or "the Synoptic Sayings Gospel." This is not because we know the title of Q. In ancient documents titles were normally found either at the beginning or end of the document. If Q had a title, it was no doubt eliminated when it was incorporated by Matthew and Luke. It is in fact very unlikely that Q called itself a "gospel" (*euaggelion*), for the simple reason that in the first century, this term was not yet the designation of a literary genre. Rather, an *euaggelion* was a message of the decisive transformation of human life. This is the very term that was used in an inscription from the Asian city of Priene, dated to 9 BCE, describing the message of a golden age that the emperor Augustus was believed to have inaugurated.[24] By this standard, Q, with its announcement of the advent of the reign of God, is every bit as much a gospel as the canonical Gospels and the message that Paul describes as his *euaggelion*. Moreover, Q refers to Jesus' proclamation to the poor with the verbal form *euaggelizesthai*, "to proclaim good news" (Q 7:22). So to refer to Q as the Sayings Gospel Q is to claim that it, no less than the more familiar Gospels of the New Testament, represents a message of a definitive transformation of human affairs, effected by God, and connected with the person of Jesus.

As I shall argue in the next chapter, we now know that there were multiple "gospels" among the Jesus movements: not only Paul's gospel, and the gospel messages preserved in the Synoptic Gospels and John, but other documents that explicitly called themselves "gospels": the *Gospel of Thomas*, the *Gospel of Philip*, the *Gospel of Truth*, and so on. So when *we* call Q a "gospel," it is to make the point that Q deserves to be considered as a decisive proclamation of a new state of affairs for humans, not simply relegated to the status of a "source" of Matthew and Luke.

Chapter Three

What a Difference Difference Makes

The reconstruction of Q results in a document, probably composed in the Galilee, and consisting of about 4,500 words of text—a document about the size of Paul's second letter to the Corinthians. But why should anyone be interested in this document, except source critics who study the ways in which Matthew and Luke composed their Gospels? Q, after all, contains *nothing* besides what we already know from Matthew and Luke, since it is reconstructed from Matthew and Luke. There are no new sayings of Jesus in it, no new stories, no new christological titles or terms that we have not already heard from Matthew and Luke. Unlike the *Gospel of Thomas* or the *Gospel of Judas*, which bring to light new sayings and stories, Q is not a new discovery.

The importance of Q lies not in any new material but rather in the distinctive manner in which it frames and presents its sayings and stories. Q is also distinctive for what it *lacks*. In Q we get a glimpse of a very early phase of the Jesus tradition that had not yet acquired the features with which we are now so familiar. So while we don't get anything new in Q, what we get is a very different formulation and arrangement of the sayings that we know from much later writings. We also have a document that lies behind the canonical Gospels and behaves differently from them. This makes a difference. Let me offer an analogy.

In 1916 German physicist Karl Schwarzschild began manipulating gravitational equations. He suggested the theoretical possibility of a stellar body that emitted no light because its mass and gravitational forces were so great that it would take particles traveling faster than the speed of light to escape its gravitational field. Since no particle travels faster than the speed of light, nothing could escape from such a star, not even light. Schwarzschild calculated that if the radius of a stellar body collapsed to a certain size (now called its Schwarzschild radius), the radiation it emitted could never escape the star's gravity. Nearby matter and energy would be sucked into this collapsing star. The density of such a stellar body would be fantastic: a star with the mass of our sun would be shrunk to about three kilometers in radius from its current radius of about 700,000 kilometers. If Earth were to be shrunk to the same density, it would have a radius of only nine millimeters! As it turns out, our sun could never become a "Schwarzschild singularity." It would have to be about four times as large as it is to have the gravitational force to collapse in this way. If it did, however, Schwarzschild's calculations indicate that the orbits of our planets would not be affected. The gravitational force that keeps them in orbit would still be in effect. But we would be circling around an unseen spot in space.

These calculations remained in the realm of theory until 1970, when astronomers observed a strong X-ray source in the constellation Cygnus. It came from a nearby blue supergiant known as HDE 226868, which also had a peculiar wobbling orbit, caused, apparently, by an unseen companion star, smaller than the earth in radius but with a mass of seven to thirteen times that of our sun. The X-ray emissions were produced not from this unseen companion, but from gasses being stripped off the supergiant by this unseen body and accelerated into an otherwise invisible location in space. Although this mysterious body could not be seen, because it emitted no light or other electromagnetic radiation, it eclipsed the blue supergiant when it passed in front, as it did every 5.6 days. With this observation, it seemed that there was now confirmation of the actual existence of a Schwarzschild singularity, christened Cygnus X-1, the first known black hole.

The idea of a black hole has had enormous appeal to science fiction writers and to television shows such as *Star Trek*. But to physicists the notion of a singularity hidden by an "event horizon," the Schwarzschild radius below which nothing could escape a star's gravity, not only made sense of the odd orbital movements of certain visible stars and strange X-ray emissions; it turns out to have much broader theoretical implications for cosmology, the history of the universe and of its stars, and the geometry of space. The postulation and eventual discovery of black holes was not simply a matter of adding yet another kind of star to our already long catalogue of previously known heavenly bodies. It is not that black holes are made of a new stellar substance; they consist of the same elements found in other stars, mostly hydrogen and helium. But black holes behaved as no other star did. Their existence changed the way in which we think about space-time.

If the idea of black holes changes our way of thinking about space-time, the origins of the universe, and its future, the idea of a lost sayings source Q also changes the way we think about Christian origins. Q is an unseen force behind the composition of Matthew and Luke. If it existed, we will have to think differently about how the earliest followers of Jesus began to enact "the kingdom of God" and how they thought about the significance of Jesus. Why? It is because Q represents a *different* type of gospel from the canonical Gospels of Matthew, Mark, Luke, and John and different again from the gospel preached by Paul. With Q, the landscape of the early Jesus movement becomes more complex.

Q allows us to see Christian origins in new perspectives, to draw new connections, to see historical developments in a different light. Features of the early Jesus that once seemed odd may seem less odd now. For example, the complete lack of reference to the saving acts of Jesus in the letter of James and the absence of any reference to the cross and resurrection have struck commentators as peculiar. But if Q also lacks any explicit reference to Jesus' crucifixion, focusing instead on his teachings, then James's silences about Jesus' death and resurrection may not be so singular. Conversely, features of early Christian literature that seemed expected, virtually inevitable—for example, that every account of Jesus' significance would necessarily include his baptism and end with the crucifixion and resurrection—will now seem less self-evident, for Q lacks any explicit description of Jesus' death. The fact that an account of Jesus' death is *not* an inevitable part of a gospel helps us appreciate even more the literary and theological achievement of Mark, who created an account of Jesus' death and gave it theological intelligibility.

The existence of Q, as a *different* gospel, is of importance because it highlights, on the one hand, the variety of literary and theological expressions that existed within the earliest Jesus movement. On the other hand, it sets in sharper relief the literary and theological choices made by Mark and his successors in framing their story of Jesus. I cannot here give a full list of the respects in which Q is different from the Synoptic Gospels, but I shall discuss five striking features of Q that distinguish it from Mark and its Synoptic successors, Matthew and Luke: (1) the role of geography and topography in the organization of Q; (2) the function and significance of the miraculous; (3) Q's silence on Jesus' death and its view of Jesus' significance; (4) Q's understanding of Jesus' vindication, and (5) Q's concrete ethics.

A Rural, Judean Gospel

When Q is compared with Mark certain features immediately become obvious. First, while Mark provides a continuous, if not entirely coherent, narrative reaching from John's baptizing activity to the discovery of Jesus' empty tomb, Q does not offer a continuous narrative at all. To be sure, Q also begins with John's activities in "all the circuit of the Jordan" (3:3) and continues with a glimpse of Jesus being tested (4:1–13). It perhaps had a reference to Jesus either entering or (more likely) leaving his hometown of Nazareth, which Q calls Nazara (4:16). But it would be impossible from Q to trace Jesus' continuous geographical movements.

The simplest explanation of the differences between Q and Mark is that Q is a *sayings gospel* while Mark is a narrative gospel. Q is closer in form to the *Gospel of Thomas* than it is to the intracanonical gospels. Its closest generic companions are not biographies like Philostratus's *Life of Apollonios of Tyana*, an account of an ancient miracle worker which resembles Mark's Gospel in significant ways. Q more closely resembles Lucian of Samosata's *Demonax*, which is a long series of anecdotes, called *chriae*, about this philosopher without a continuous narrative framework, or the "Chapters of the Fathers" (*m. 'Abot*) in the Mishnah, a collection of sayings and *chriae* of various early rabbis with virtually no narrative framework apart from a brief "genealogy" of the students of Rabbi Yohanan ben Zakkai.

Q, however, is not a formless collection of bare maxims and *chriae*. On the contrary, the framers of Q have organized its contents into several discursive units, each furnished with a description of the occasion or the audience of the speech. John's preaching (3:7b–9, 16–17) is contextualized as speech delivered to crowds coming out to him (3:7a); the disciples are the recipients of Jesus' first speech (6:20a), which concludes with Jesus entering Capernaum where he encounters a centurion (7:1a). Jesus' sayings about John are told to the crowds that had "gone out" to see John (7:24a), while the speech on mission (10:2–16) is precipitated by two (or three) would-be disciples approaching Jesus (9:57–60 ‹61–62›). The mission speech concludes with Jesus spontaneously praising God "in that hour" (10:22a), which then leads to an instruction on prayer (11:2–4, 9–13). Q uses a brief exorcism story (11:14) to introduce the Beelzebul accusation and the request for a sign (11:15–26, 29–32), and interjects into this sequence an episode where a woman cries out from the crowd, flattering Jesus (11:27–28). There may have been more of these brief transitional introductions in the rest of Q, but the editing of Q by Matthew and Luke has likely effaced them. What is clear is that Q *does* organize sayings by discursive settings—speech to crowds, to disciples, to opponents, to others—although it does not attempt to fully narrativize its account.

Mark uses geography to organize an itinerary for Jesus. He begins in the Jordan valley, with John, moves to Capernaum, then across the Kinneret (Sea of Galilee) into the Decapolis, up to Tyre and Sidon and Caesarea Philippi, and then through the Galilee and on to Jerusalem. Q also uses geographical locations—Sodom,

Jerusalem, Nazara, Capernaum, Bethsaida, Khorazin, Tyre, Sidon, and Nineveh—but not as points on which to plot the movements of its dramatis personae. Instead, Q uses these locations as *symbolic sites*, representing places of devastating judgment (Sodom) and of the rejection of the prophets (Jerusalem), sites where the Jesus people were rejected (Capernaum, Bethsaida, Khorazin), and Gentile cities whose inhabitants are imagined to stand in judgment over "this generation," Q's code word for its contemporaries. The arid and inhospitable wasteland of the Jordan rift valley, with its bituminous stench, still recalls the story of the destroyed city of Sodom; but it is also where one "goes out to see" a man who is even "more than a prophet" (7:25–26). There are houses and villages where healing and the proclamation of the kingdom of God are experienced and where "children of peace" may be found (10:5–9). But markets, palaces, plazas, and assemblies—interestingly, all public spaces—are the places on the map where Q anticipates strife, arrogance, and false discipleship (7:25, 31; 11:43; 13:26). Towns such as Capernaum—the town that Mark and Matthew think of as Jesus' adoptive hometown and the location of Simon's house—are arrogant and apparently unwelcoming to the Jesus people (10:13–15).

Q then uses geography and topography not to map movement but to delineate where friends of the kingdom may be found and where opposition or indifference lies. Once Q was incorporated into Matthew and Luke, who use geography very differently, Q's distinctive "symbolic topography" was obscured from view.

There are two even more important consequences of Matthew and Luke's editing. First, Matthew and Luke are Gospels oriented to *urban* settings. Matthew assumes a world in which traveling magi come to visit a king (and are surprised that the king is in fact born in a small town). Matthew's Jerusalem is called "the holy city" (4:5) and the "city of the Great King" (5:35). It is a world where kings make gigantic loans or entrust retainers with huge sums of gold (18:23–35; 25:14–30). In Matthew's spatial imagination, the city is at the center. In his parable of the Wedding Banquet (22:1–10) Matthew also portrays a king sending out his servants even "into the main roads out of the city" (*tas diexodous ton hodon*) in order to invite guests to a feast (22:9). It is where kings sit in judgment over subjects (25:31–46). These are all urban images. Luke, of course, lives in a world of cities too. His Gospel is centered on Jerusalem and its temple: this is where his Gospel begins, with an angel appearing to Zechariah, and where it ends, with the disciples remaining in Jerusalem and daily visiting its temple. And of course in Acts, Paul moves from city to city in Asia and Greece, establishing churches. He pays no attention at all to the countryside.

In Q, by contrast, the countryside and private spaces—villages and their houses, and the wasteland—are the points on Q's "map" privileged with belief and the embrace of the kingdom of God. Cities are places where Q can expect rejection, arrogance, or indifference. The way in which Q imagines the places where the kingdom is embraced is very different from the ways in which Matthew and Luke, in their world of cities, imagine the presence of the kingdom. If we had only Matthew and Luke, we would not see this face of the Jesus movement, the face of its earliest embodiment in the villages and towns of Galilee.

Second, whereas Luke's world is the world of the Gentile cities of the eastern Mediterranean, and eventually, Rome, Q's world is centered in the Galilee, on the towns of Capernaum, Bethsaida, Khorazin, and Nazara, the latter two so small and insignificant that they did not merit mention in the Hebrew Bible or in Josephus's writings. Q's world is a Jewish or "Judean" world where Gentiles are on the periphery—to the north in Tyre and Sidon (Q 10:13–14) or the extreme north in Nineveh (Q 11:32). Gentiles make appearances in Q but they are exceptional: a centurion (probably imagined to be a Roman) meets Jesus and expresses a surprising confidence in Jesus (Q 7:1–10). Q in fact tells the story of this centurion precisely because his confidence is so exceptional and because it puts to shame those who in Q's view ought to have confidence in Jesus.

In contrast to Mark's Gospel, Q contains no controversies over Sabbath violations (compare Mark 2:23–38; 3:1–6) or disputes about *kashrut* (food laws; Mark 7:15–23). In contrast to Luke, there is no anticipation that Judeans would give up the observance of their table practices, as Acts 10 seems to enjoin. Nor does Q question the practice of circumcision, a key topic of Paul's letter to the Galatians and of Acts 15. This is probably because Q presupposed an exclusively Israelite environment where people naturally circumcised their sons, kept *kashrut*, and observed the Sabbath. There was indeed no reason *not* to observe these commandments. Q's complaint with other Jewish groups is not that they observed the Torah and the Q people did not. Rather, Q's complaint against the Pharisees—no doubt, a bit of caricature—is that they insist on one set of commandments and neglect others:

> [42]Woe for you, Pharisees, for you tithe mint and dill and cumin, and [[give up]] justice and mercy and faithfulness. *But these one has to do, without giving up those.* [39b]Woe to you, Pharisees, for you purify the outside of the cup and dish, but inside [[they are]] full of plunder and dissipation. [41][[Purify]] . . . the inside of the cup, «and» its outside «will be» pure. (Q 11:42, 39b–41)

Q acknowledges that tithing and purifications are valid—«but these one has to do, without giving up those»—but insists that other values are central to the Torah.[1]

In other words Q presents us with a rural, Galilean Jewish gospel, not a gospel that already imagines the extension of the mission of the Jesus movement to Gentile areas and the cultic debates that this extension would provoke. It is this feature of Q that is perhaps the most significant, since along with the letter of James, Q provides us with one of the very few arguable instances of a document produced by and for the earliest Judean followers of Jesus.

Miracles and the Kingdom of God

Another feature of Q becomes obvious when it is compared with Mark. Mark's Gospel is dominated by miracle stories and exorcisms, all designed to raise the question, "Who is Jesus?" The demons immediately identify Jesus as the son of God, but Mark's disciples, who witness all of Jesus' wonders, are so painfully slow in coming to an awareness of Jesus' identity that it is not until half way through the Gospel, after a long series of wondrous events, that Peter is able to venture a partial identification, "You are the Christ" (Mark 8:29). Even at the dramatic stilling of the storm the disciples ask, "Who is it that even the winds and sea obey him?"— unknowingly paraphrasing the Psalms in which God is depicted as the one who commands the wind and sea.[2] If they had only listened to their own words, they would know that Jesus must be God's son. But this is only half of Jesus' identity; he is also the Son of Man who must suffer, an identity that the disciples never seem to grasp. Ironically, it is not one of the disciples who first grasps Jesus' full identity, but a Roman and a centurion who first declares what Mark's readers were told at the very beginning (1:1): "Truly this man is a son of God" (15:39).

Miracles are numerically less prominent in Q. But this does not mean that Q denies or ignores them. Rather, Q simply takes miracles for granted. There are only two miracle stories, the healing of a centurion's serving boy in Capernaum (Q 7:1–10) and an exorcism (11:14). In neither case does Q's interest lie in the miraculous as a *demonstration* of Jesus' identity. Rather, Q is interested in the *speech* or *teaching* that Jesus' miracles occasion. The focus of attention in Q 7:1–10 is the centurion's rather matter-of-fact grasp of Jesus' authority and Jesus' declaration about this Gentile, "I tell you, not even in Israel have I found such faith" (7:9). The point is not so much belief in some special identity of Jesus, whether as Christ or son of God or Son of Man, but instead the centurion's understanding that wonders can be seen if one believes. As Q later says, "If you have faith like a mustard seed, you might say to this mulberry tree: Be uprooted and planted in the sea! And it would obey you" (17:6).

For Q, wonders are connected with the advent of the kingdom. When John asks Jesus' identity, "Are you the one to come?" (7:19), Jesus responds by pointing to a number of wonders—healings, the raising of the dead, and preaching to the poor (7:22). There is not even a direct claim that *only* Jesus performs such wonders. The point is that wonders are occurring, and this means that the one to come has arrived. In his answer to opponents seeking a sign, Jesus declares that "there is some*thing* greater than Solomon and Jonah here" (11:31–32), not some*one*. Q's emphasis is on the presence of the kingdom of God, of which Jesus is a special envoy, of course. But it is the kingdom that is the transformative power in people's lives.

The other miracle, Q 11:14, is used not to prove Jesus' identity, but rather to show how the miraculous is inherently ambiguous. Jesus' opponents witness the exorcism and conclude that it was effected through collusion with Beelzebul, a derogatory name for a Phoenician deity which came to be associated with the demonic. Jesus' retort argues that this is not a coherent conclusion: exorcisms cannot be effected by the demonic, and in any case would the opponents draw the same conclusion about other Judean exorcists? (11:19). Of course they would not. For Q it is not the raw demonstration of power that points ineluctably to the significance of Jesus and the kingdom; rather, it is the power of *logic* and *wisdom* which ought to lead those amenable to reason to conclude that God's reign "has come upon you" (11:20). Jesus demonstrates the presence of the kingdom by an argument. The fact that Q does not privilege wonders is shown by the next pericope, where opponents seek a sign. Jesus refuses such a demonstration on the grounds that they have *already* received a sign comparable to "the sign of Jonah" (11:30). This sign is not the resurrection of Jesus, as Matthew tries to interpret it (Matt. 12:40). We might suppose that events such as those enumerated in Q 7:22 ought to lead the person of insight to belief. But in this controversy, Q seems to be pointing to other events that ought to lead a person of insight to acknowledge the reign of God. Q adduces the example of the Queen of the South and the people of Nineveh, neither of whom witnessed miracles, but nonetheless recognized God's power in Solomon and Jonah. Q argues that "there is some-*thing* greater than Solomon or Jonah here" (11:31–32).

The signs of the kingdom, then, are much wider than simply miracles. They can be found in the everyday, in the activities of birds and lilies (12:22–31), and in welcoming the Q people to a village (10:6–9). Q indeed is a bit reticent when it comes to wonders and signs:

[20][[«But on being asked when the kingdom of God is coming, he answered them and said: The kingdom of God is not coming visibly.»]] [21][[«Nor will one say:» Look, here! or: «There! For, look, the kingdom of God is among you!»]] (Q 17:20–21)

Q's treatment of wonders anticipates that found later in the Fourth Gospel. John also refuses to endorse miracles as an unassailable proof of Jesus' identity or as the foundation of adequate belief. The risen Johannine Jesus' response to "doubting" Thomas is emblematic: "Because you have seen me you believe; blessed are those who do not see and yet believe" (John 20:29). For John, miracles are not transparent; on the contrary, they are open to divergent and contradictory interpretations. Only those who have received the Spirit are capable of "seeing" Jesus' deeds as they are truly meant to be seen. Of course Q has not yet articulated the epistemological dualism that is characteristic of the Fourth Gospel, where those born of God understand all and those born of the devil live in darkness. But Q shares with the Fourth Gospel a sapiential epistemology also found in the wisdom books of the Mediterranean. The sage, examining the world and the events of the world, is able to perceive what is not immediately evident to most: the presence of God's designs and God's reign.

Again, we must note that Q's distinctive treatment of the miraculous was hidden from view once it was embedded in Matthew and Luke. Matthew treats miracles as "the deeds of the Christ" (11:2), acts which point to and prove Jesus' messianic identity. Luke, speaking through one of his characters in Acts, describes Jesus as a man who "went about doing good (*euergetein*) and healing all who were oppressed by the devil, for God was with him" (Acts 10:38). That is, Luke presents Jesus as a *benefactor* and uses the technical Greek term *euergetein*, "to be a benefactor." For Luke, too, Jesus' wondrous deeds point inevitably to a single interpretation. What is lost is Q's sapiential approach not only to wonders but to perception in general. It is the sage, preeminently Jesus but also the Jesus people—who can see the presence of the reign of God in events that others treat as ordinary, demonic, or just puzzling.

Jesus' Death in Q

Perhaps the most striking difference between Q and the Synoptic Gospels is its lack of an explicit narration of Jesus' death and resurrection. Before the discovery of the *Gospel of Thomas* scholars took for granted that Jesus' death was the one critical datum that every early Christian Gospel writer would narrate and interpret. For that reason, few before the 1950s dared to call Q a "gospel," since it lacked what was deemed essential to any gospel. Q could only be conceived of as a supplement, intended for those who already knew the story of Jesus' passion and resurrection. This in turn presupposed a hierarchy of Christian beliefs—those beliefs that were essential to Christian belief and others that were derivative or supplementary. As T. W. Manson put it in an essay originally published in 1937,

> [f]or the primitive Church the central thing is the Cross on the Hill rather than the Sermon on the Mount. . . . Christian doctrine and Christian ethics may be the inevitable corollaries of the Christian gospel; but they are corollaries.[3]

The core of the beliefs of the Jesus movement could *only* rest on an interpretation of Jesus' death. All else was supplementary elaboration. B. H. Streeter could imagine a function for Q only if it presupposed a Palestinian passion tradition; for him, Q was a handbook for missionaries who had already embraced the passion *kerygma*.[4]

Even B. W. Bacon, one of the few in the 1920s to actually call Q a "gospel," did so because he assumed that Q already contained an interpretation of Jesus' death in the form of a quotation of Isaiah 42:1–4, which he ascribed to Q. According to Bacon, Q was not merely a sayings collection, but

> a presentation of the *kind of ministry* represented by Jesus' career, a true *Gospel* . . . , in which Jesus was set forth as the redeeming "Wisdom" of God, the Suffering Servant of Isaian prophecy [Isa. 42:1–4], humbled in obedience unto

rejection and death and, therefore, also "highly exalted." It will have been a gospel more akin to Paul and John than many of our extant Synoptics.[5]

The discovery of the *Gospel of Thomas* in 1945 changed this kind of thinking. Thomas contains no narrative at all, only 114 sayings, without any references to or interpretation of Jesus' death. Yet it calls itself a gospel (*euaggelion*). Thus, it seems clear that a gospel need not contain a passion narrative or even a continuous narrative. It is true that there are really two titles for Thomas: the title "The Gospel according to Thomas" that appears in the colophon, and another in the opening words, preserved in both Coptic and in an early third-century Greek fragment (*Papyrus Oxyrhynchus* IV 654.1–5): "These are the hidden words (*logoi*) which the Living Jesus spoke and which Judas, also called Thomas, wrote down." Even if, as seems likely, the title in the colophon is not the original title but was added later, it is nonetheless the case that an editor thought that a collection of Jesus' *logoi* qualified as a gospel.

If Thomas was a gospel, offering a distinctive perspective on the saving significance of Jesus and his words, but without any reference to Jesus' death, then it would seem that Q might also be considered to be a gospel rather than a catechetical supplement to the Passion kerygma. But it would raise another even more consequential possibility. In contrast to Manson's belief, the "Cross on the Hill" was not inevitably the center and heart of all Christian theologizing. Other perspectives were not only possible, but in fact, Thomas attests to such a possibility.

Some of the earlier treatments of Q tried to solve the problem of Q's lack of any reference to Jesus' death simply by asserting that as a sayings collection containing sapiential and prophetic sayings, there is really no place to represent Jesus' death. After all, the collection is framed not as a retrospective narrative about Jesus, but rather *as if* it is the voice of the living Jesus. To include material about Jesus' death would seem artificial and anachronistic. Of course, this did not stop Mark from including sayings of Jesus in which he predicted his arrest and death at the hands of Gentiles (Mark 8:31; 9:31; 10:32–34, 45). Q, as far as it can be reconstructed, contains no such predictions.

The situation is a bit more complicated. Despite the fact that Q lacks a narrative of Jesus' death or sayings that refer specifically to his death, Q is not as silent as some might suppose. But we must distinguish between whether Q has a passion story or even knows of the passion kerygma of 1 Corinthians 15:3b–5—there is no evidence of this—and whether there are any reflections on Jesus' death.[6] In fact, Q has some elements which point toward a construal of Jesus' death.

One of Q's sayings is "The one who does not take one's cross and follow after me cannot be my disciple" (Q 14:27). Does this presuppose knowledge of a passion narrative or even recall the story of Simon of Cyrene carrying Jesus' cross? Probably not. Nothing in Q 14:27 itself makes the connection: Q speaks of the disciple "*receiving* (*lambanein*) his [own] cross" and "following after," while Mark's description of Simon in Mark 15:21 uses "*lift up* (*airein*) his [Jesus'] cross" but makes no mention of Simon *following* Jesus. Even Mark has not bothered to assimilate his story of Simon to his own version of the cross saying (Mark 8:38).[7] Nevertheless, it is hard to imagine that the Q people, hearing Q 14:27, would not connect it somehow with Jesus' death. More than this, the saying suggests that discipleship be seen as inextricably connected with the willingness to undergo a shameful death such as that endured by Jesus. This does not make Jesus' death salvific, but it does imply that Jesus' fate was understood by Q as an integral part of his identity and activity.

Another saying that suggests that the Q people were able to offer a construal of Jesus' death is Q 6:22–23:

> Blessed are you when they insult and [[persecute]] you, and [[say every kind of]] evil [[against]] you because of the son of man. Be glad and [[exult]], for vast is your recompense in heaven. For this is how they [[persecuted]] the prophets who «were» before you.

While not expressly speaking of Jesus, this beatitude describes the ill treatment that Jesus' followers endure "because of the son of man." The final clause draws a connection between this suffering and the treatment of the prophets.

What Q invokes here is called the "Deuteronomistic view of the prophets," frequently attested in Jeremiah and some of the later books of the Hebrew Bible and in Second Temple literature. In this theology, the history of Israel is depicted as a repetitive cycle of sinfulness, prophetic calls to repentance (which are ignored), punishment by God, and renewed calls to repentance with threats of judgment. Common in this schema is the motif of the rejection of the prophets and even of their murder. This may seem odd, since the Hebrew Bible itself records no story of the murder of a prophet, except Elijah's killing of the prophets of Ba'al. Books such as Isaiah and Amos generally depict prophets as critics of the monarchy and as advocates of social reforms. In Deuteronomistic theology, however, the prophets are represented primarily as *preachers of repentance* and as *rejected preachers*.[8]

Thus, when the persecution of the prophets is mentioned in Q 6:22–23, Deuteronomistic theology is invoked. It does not require too much imagination to suppose that the beatitude also has Jesus' fate in view and, like 14:27, associates the disciples' fates with that of their teacher. This does not make Jesus' death salvific any more than the prophets' deaths are salvific. But it does mean that Q viewed Jesus' fate as inextricably related to his other activities and asserts that discipleship involves a mimesis of Jesus' behavior and character.

This is not the only point where Q invokes Deuteronomistic theology. We find it again at 11:47–51:

> Woe to you, for you built the tombs of the prophets, but your «fore»fathers killed them. «Thus» [[you]] witness [[against yourselves that]] you are [[sons]] of your «fore»fathers. Therefore also the Wisdom said: I will send them prophets and sages, and «some» of them they will kill and persecute, so that «a settling of accounts for» the blood of all the prophets poured out from the founding of the world may be

required of this generation, from «the» blood of Abel to «the» blood of Zechariah, murdered between the sacrificial altar and the House. Yes, I tell you, «an accounting» will be required of this generation!

Q here repeats a common refrain of Deuteronomistic theology, that the rejection of the prophets will provoke divine punishment. See, for example, Nehemiah's prayer in Nehemiah 9:24, 26–27:

> [24]So the [Israelites] went in and possessed the land, and you subdued before them the inhabitants of the land, the Canaanites, and gave them into their hands, with their kings and the peoples of the land, to do with them as they pleased. . . . [26]Nevertheless they were disobedient and rebelled against you and cast your law behind their backs and *killed your prophets*, who had warned them in order to turn them back to you, and they committed great blasphemies. [27]Therefore you gave them into the hands of their enemies, who made them suffer.

Deuteronomistic theology appears again at Q 13:34–35:

> O Jerusalem, Jerusalem, who kills the prophets and stones those sent to her! How often I wanted to gather your children together, as a hen gathers her nestlings under her wings, and you were not willing! Look, your house is forsaken! I tell you, you will not see me until [[«the time» comes when]] you say: Blessed is the one who comes in the name of the Lord!

Deuteronomistic theology is in fact so frequent in Q that we must conclude that the framers of Q used this theological pattern as a key way to think about their own experience of marginalization (see Q 6:22–23) and doubtless about Jesus' own fate. As one who called Israel to repentance, Jesus too could expect to suffer the fate of a prophet. This is probably the way that the Q people regarded John as well. For Q, John is primarily a repentance preacher (3:7–9) and he, along with Jesus, is rejected by "this generation" (7:33–34):

> For John came, neither eating nor drinking, and you say: He
> has a demon! The son of man came, eating and drinking, and
> you say: Look! A person «who is» a glutton and drunkard, a
> friend of tax collectors and sinners! But Wisdom was vindicated by her children.

Hence, Q is not without a view of Jesus' death, although we do not find an explicit narration of his death. Instead, Q sees Jesus' death through the lens of the Deuteronomistic view of the prophets, whose fate it was to be rejected, and even killed. Jesus, John, and the Q people belong to the same lineage, and therefore can expect to suffer as did the prophets. They remain, nevertheless, God's envoys, vindicated in God's sight.

When Q was incorporated into Matthew and Luke, the centrality of Deuteronomistic theology as an explanation of Jesus' death was muffled significantly. Instead, Matthew emphasized the expiatory nature of Jesus' death. At the Last Supper Jesus states:

> This is my blood of the covenant which is poured out for
> many *for the forgiveness of sins.* (Matt. 26:28)

Matthew, moreover, depicts Jesus' death as an apocalyptic event, complete with an earthquake that split rocks, opened tombs, and awoke many dead holy ones. This recalls Ezekiel's vision in Ezekiel 37 of the time when God would reconstitute Israel and infuse the people with his Spirit. For Matthew, Jesus' death is the moment of the turning of the ages and the beginning of the renewal of Israel.

Luke is more amenable to the Deuteronomistic view of the prophets. The Lukan Jesus, responding to the Pharisees' warning to stay away from Jerusalem and Herod Antipas, declares,

> Go and tell that fox for me, "Listen, I am casting out demons
> and performing cures today and tomorrow, and on the third

day I finish my work. Yet today, tomorrow, and the next day I must be on my way, because it is impossible for a prophet to be killed outside of Jerusalem." (Luke 13:32–33)

In Acts Stephen's speech to his opponents directly adduces Deuteronomistic theology:

You stiff-necked people, uncircumcised in heart and ears, you are forever opposing the Holy Spirit, just as your ancestors used to do. Which of the prophets did your ancestors not persecute? They killed those who foretold the coming of the Righteous One, and now you have become his betrayers and murderers. (Acts 7:51–52)

Yet the dominant theology of Jesus' death in Luke is that of an innocent sufferer, indeed, a *noble death*. Jesus may be a prophet who suffers a prophet's fate, but preeminently he is a hero who dies in control of his faculties, dies as a rational man, dies courageously like Socrates, not railing against his enemies but forgiving them. Thus Luke's Jesus embodies the Greek ideal of the hero who is not reduced to the subhuman by death, but meets death honorably.[9]

We could continue to elaborate the differences between the Synoptics and Q on the topic of Jesus' death, but there is one important similarity. As I have suggested above in connection with Q 6:22–23 and 14:27, Q does not regard Jesus' fate as something extraneous to his identity or as an accident. Like Mark and his successors, Q insists that Jesus' fate is *integral* to his identity and that, correspondingly, those who imitate Jesus as followers must likewise be prepared to suffer as he did: "The one who does not take one's cross and follow after me cannot be my disciple" (14:27). Although it was not inevitable that an account of Jesus' activities and sayings would always feature a passion narrative—and some early Christian writings such as the *Gospel of Thomas* did not treat Jesus' death in any way—Q does offer a construal of Jesus' death. But it is quite different from the construals that eventually formed the Synoptic Gospels, based not on the concept of expiation or a noble death, but on the Deuteronomistic model of the prophet's death.

Is Jesus Raised?

The notion of the resurrection of Jesus is so ubiquitous in early Christian literature that it is hard to imagine any writer either ignoring it or having a different view. The resurrection of Jesus is fundamental to Paul's thinking, for he views it as a cosmic event and a paradigmatic event in which the believer may participate through faith. Without the resurrection, there would be no Pauline theology. Predictions of Jesus' resurrection are also integral to the fabric of Mark's Gospel (8:31; 9:31; 10:32–34; 14:28; 16:7), and these predictions are developed into full-scale resurrection appearance stories in Matthew and Luke.

The concept of resurrection derives from the conviction among many Judeans that the human person was not divisible into an immortal soul and a mortal body but was a single unified being. This implied that if there was to be any continuation of human existence after death, it would necessarily involve a body. Even the final judgment required resurrection:

> And many of those who sleep in the dust of the earth shall awake, some to everlasting life and some to shame and everlasting contempt. Those who are wise shall shine like the brightness of the sky; and those who turn many to righteousness, like the stars for ever and ever. (Dan. 12:2–3)

Even Paul, who shows the influence of Greek ideas, was still committed to the idea of a resurrection body, though he insisted that the resurrection body was a "spiritual body" (1 Cor. 15).

The Sayings Gospel Q also invokes the idea of resurrection in several contexts, but it is not Jesus' resurrection that is in focus. In Q 7:22, one of the indications that the One to Come is here is the raising of the dead:

> Go report to John what you hear and see: The blind regain their sight and the lame walk around, the skin-diseased are cleansed and the deaf hear, and dead are raised (*nekroi egeirontai*), and the poor are given good news. (Q 7:22)

This is in fact a pastiche of quotations from Isaiah which look forward to a time of redemption.[10] A similar pastiche appears in a fragmentary text from Qumran, which also connects resurrection with the end times:

> [the hea]vens and the earth will listen to His Messiah, and none therein will stray from the commandments of the holy ones. Seekers of the Lord, strengthen yourselves in His service! All you hopeful in (your) heart, will you not find the Lord in this? For the Lord will consider the pious (*hasidim*) and call the righteous by name. Over the poor His spirit will hover and will renew the faithful with His power. And He will glorify the pious on the throne of the eternal Kingdom. He who liberates the captives, *restores sight to the blind*, straightens the b[ent]. And f[or] ever I will cleav[e to the h]opeful and in His mercy . . . And the fr[uit . . .] will not be delayed for anyone. And the Lord will accomplish glorious things which have never been as [He . . .] For He will heal the wounded, and *make the dead to live* and *bring good news to the poor*. . . . He will lead the uprooted and knowledge . . . and smoke (?) (4Q521)

It is not clear whether these deeds are supposed to be deeds of the Messiah or actions of God connected with the appearance of the Messiah, but neither is it clear whether Q 7:22 describes *Jesus'* deeds or deeds that surround the appearance of the One to Come. In either case, however, 4Q521 and Q 7:22 connect the healing of the blind and lame, raising of the dead, and bringing good news to the poor with the advent of a messianic age. Neither text, however, suggests that the Messiah or the One to Come will himself rise from the dead.

Resurrection also appears in Q at Q 11:31–32, in Jesus' retort to those seeking a sign:

> The queen of the South will be raised (*egerthesetai*) at the judgment with this generation and condemn it, for she came from the ends of the earth to listen to the wisdom of Solomon,

and look, something more than Solomon is here! Ninevite
men will arise (*anastesontai*) at the judgment with this generation and condemn it. For they repented at the preaching of
Jonah, and look, something more than Jonah is here!

Q here reflects the widespread belief in Second Temple
Judaism that a general resurrection will precede God's judgment
(e.g., Dan. 12:2–3). Again, it is not Jesus' resurrection that is at
issue, but the resurrection of two Gentile witnesses against "this
generation."

If Q was well aware of the concept of resurrection, why is there
no hint of it in connection with the fate of Jesus? As I have argued
above, the Q people regarded death as intrinsic to Jesus' identity
as their model and ideal. Is it possible that they simply believed
that Jesus, like the prophets killed before him, would have to await
the general resurrection for vindication? But this would imply that
the Q folk were sufficiently cut off from other early streams of the
Jesus movement that they had not heard of the tales of the empty
tomb or the appearances of Jesus to his followers. This scenario is
indeed difficult to imagine.

Why, then, if Q was well aware of the concept of resurrection,
did it not extend this to Jesus? The answer may lie in the possibility, recently defended by Daniel Smith,[11] that in order to
understand Jesus' postmortem vindication, Q did not use the
metaphor of resurrection—the revivification of a corpse—but the
metaphor of *assumption*, the taking up of the righteous.

Like the concept of resurrection, the notion of assumption also
depends on a belief in the unity of the human person. If a person
is to be caught up to heaven, it cannot merely be the "soul" or
"mind." It must involve the entire person. In the Bible both Elijah and Enoch were said to have been removed to heaven prior to
their natural deaths. The terminology most commonly associated
with the assumption of a figure has to do with being "removed
from sight": he disappears, no longer appears, and no longer is
seen.[12] As 2 Kings 2:12 states, Elisha "no longer saw [Elijah]" (*kai
ouk eiden auton eti*). The motif of nonappearance is attested earlier

in the description of Enoch's disappearance in Genesis 5:24: "Enoch was pleasing to God and *he was not found,* for God removed him." In the account in *1 Enoch* 12:1, the writer says, "and none of the people knew where he had been taken, and where he is, or what became of him." The Wisdom of Solomon employs the same idea to describe God's deliverance of the just man from persecution:

> There was one who pleased God and was loved by him, and while living among sinners he was taken up. He was caught (*hērpagē*) up lest evil change his understanding or deceit deceive his soul. (Wis. 4:10–11)

Seen in this context, Jesus' statement in Q 13:35 that the Jerusalemites "will no longer see me" (*ou mē idēte me*) recalls the description of Elijah's or Enoch's departure. He will no longer be seen because God removed him, whether before or after death. But Q also looks forward to a future role for Jesus: "I tell you, you will not see me until [[«the time» comes when]] you say: Blessed is the one who comes in the name of the Lord!" (Q 13:35).

The premature disappearance of holy persons encouraged the expectation that they had been taken away because they had yet a future role to play. God was holding them in reserve. Hence, the widespread belief that Elijah would return to play a role in the restoration or judgment of Israel (Mal. 4:5–6; Sir. 48:10). Enoch was also expected to play a role in the future as son of man (*1 En.* 70–71), and both Baruch and Ezra were said to have been assumed to await some eschatological function.[13] The just man of the Wisdom of Solomon likewise appears in the final judgment to confound his erstwhile persecutors (Wis. 5:1–8).

Dieter Zeller noted how congenial the notion of God's rescue of an envoy was with the Deuteronomistic view of the prophets. By means of assumption, God both preserved the just from contamination (Wis. 4:11; *2 Bar.* 48.29–30) and spared them from the coming eschatological catastrophe (*4 Ezra* 14.15). Assumption and the Deuteronomistic view of the prophets are found combined in

Enoch's Animal Apocalypse (*1 En.* 85–90), where Elijah's assumption is made the *direct* result of the persecution of the prophets.[14]

If it is correct that Q 13:35 invokes the concept of *assumption* rather than resurrection, we can suggest that the Q people regarded Jesus' death as the death of a just man or a prophet whom God had "taken up," pending some future eschatological function. This accounts for the fact that Q accords Jesus' death no special salvific significance, but jumps immediately to Jesus' return as the one who is to come (11:49–51; 13:34–35). In the parallel texts from Second Temple Judaism, it was not the death of the sage that was salvific, but rather the figure's expected eschatological role that was important.

Again we should observe that when Q was incorporated into Matthew and Luke, this view of Jesus' vindication was completely obscured. Matthew and Luke employ the concept of resurrection and underscore this with stories of the appearance of the risen Jesus. If it were not for Q, we might assume that resurrection was the *only* metaphor that was used by the early Jesus movement to articulate the idea of Jesus' postmortem vindication. But if Q employed assumption theology, we might also read Mark's story of the discovery of the empty tomb in a different light. Mark, famously, has no resurrection appearance stories, only the discovery of an empty tomb. The motif of the *disappearance* of a body is closely connected with assumption theology.[15] It was only when Mark edited the empty tomb story that he had taken from earlier tradition and incorporated into his Gospel, framed with predictions of death *and resurrection* (8:31; 9:31; 10:32–34), that the empty tomb story was transformed from a story of death and disappearance into a story of death and (implied) resurrection.

We must admit that this speculation about Q's view of Jesus' vindication is based on the slenderest of evidence: half a sentence in Q 13:35. Yet what is in Q fits what we know of assumption theology and makes sense of the fact that Q does not treat Jesus' death as an expiatory sacrifice or special saving event, as do Matthew and Paul. Q again provides a *different perspective* on one of the central beliefs of Christianity. Resurrection was not the *only* metaphor available by which to imagine Jesus' postmortem vindication.

The Kingdom and Concrete Ethics

Before discussing features of Q's ethical teaching, it is necessary to say a few words about religion in the ancient Mediterranean world. In the twenty-first century we usually think of religion as a discrete and identifiable aspect of culture and distinguish it from economics, politics, education, and other cultural domains. Yet in ancient Mediterranean languages there is no word at all that is equivalent to our abstract term "religion." There are words for altars, sacrifices, prayers, and temples and words for attitudes toward the gods (piety, impiety, fear). But there was no collective word that gathers all of these into a single domain, distinguishable from the family, the city, the empire, the army, trade and professional associations, and other social institutions.

Religion in the ancient world was *embedded* in these institutions. Households honored their own patronal deities; religious practices were embedded in family life. So also with business: professional guilds of shippers were devoted to Poseidon; woodcutters' guilds worshiped Silvanus. To be a citizen of Athens meant that one had Athena as a patronal deity. Civic notables strove to obtain political offices, but they also strove to have priesthoods. Cities sponsored sacrifices, built temples, and conducted festivals. The idea of the separation of church and state was unthinkable in the ancient world. The emperor Augustus, after all, was *pontifex maximus*, the chief priest of the Roman cult. For much of history in the two centuries before the Common Era, the political ruler of Jewish Palestine was also the high priest of the Jewish cult. Even during the first century, when Judea was governed by a Roman prefect and the Galilee by a Herodian prince, the priesthood in Jerusalem was an extremely potent political force. Conversely, the temple was not just a religious site but the focal point for the collections of taxes or tithes that supported a priestly aristocracy and hence, an economic center and the focal point of economic redistribution in the form of loans and capital.[16]

Festivals were not simply religious events but were part and parcel of political, social, and economic life. Hannukah and Passover were festivals of national liberation, which also explains why Passover time in Jerusalem was explosive politically. (Jesus, it will be remembered, was executed as a messianic pretender by the Romans during Passover). The Feast of Sukkot (Tabernacles) was a harvest festival, coordinated with the olive and grape harvests, and Shavuot (Weeks) was coordinated with wheat harvest in the late spring. An index of the political importance of the cult is that the Romans, who controlled Judea, kept custody of the high priest's garments, and allowed him to use them only under their supervision. Cultic insignia and clothing were not simply fancy clothing for serving God; they carried with them social and political power that could be mobilized against Roman interests.

If religion was embedded in daily life, it functioned in the politics of the state quite differently from the religion embedded in the daily life of villagers and townsfolk. Douglas Oakman describes the difference thus:

> Religion, politics, and economics embedded within elite interests can be predicted to serve organization and legitimation of a social system to benefit those elites. Order is the primary social goal and value. Religion is shaped significantly in the direction of what Weber called a "theodicy of good fortune," a justification of the status of the elite group. Order is seen as rooted in a natural or cosmic pattern, and expressed in impersonal arrangements of political economy. . . .
>
> Non-elite interests (including both declassed elites and non-elites) embedded within elite religion, politics, and economics will either adapt to suffering through religion (Weber's "theodicy of suffering") or attempt to access collective representations without elite authorization in order to resist and even overthrow that order. Finding meaning in suffering and seeking a reordering are primary social goals and values. Reordering is legitimated through an appeal to a higher religious court, and carried through in familistic or quasi-familistic arrangements.[17]

Another way to describe the difference between the religion of the elite and that of the nonelite borrows Robert Redfield's distinction between "great" and "little" traditions. The great traditions are the learned syntheses and theologies cultivated in palace schools, temples, and among the elite. Naturally, the great tradition is formulated to sustain the economic and political interests of the elite. The little tradition represents the largely unreflective, untheologized beliefs and practices of the nonelite, found at the level of the village and town.[18]

There are both continuities and tensions between the great and little tradition. In terms of content, there is usually a considerable overlap between the great and the little tradition. The little tradition is normally dependent upon the great tradition: the syntheses of the great tradition furnish the lexicon of beliefs for the little tradition. But there is a difference in articulation: the abstract beliefs of the great tradition are usually rendered in a much more concrete form in the little tradition and are mixed with local beliefs and practices. The abstract belief in God's providence might appear at the village level as the expectation of a good harvest this year or the birth of a son. Success in the harvest or in childbirth could also be linked to devotion to a local saint, or drinking from the right well, or making the right incantations. As James Scott points out, peasants often emulate the orthodoxies of previous generations of the great tradition, from which the current ruling elite have already moved on.[19] Hence, the elite frequently regard the little tradition as quaint, unschooled, and contaminated with unorthodox beliefs and practices.

Although there is a strong correlation between the great and the little tradition, there are also tensions. The abstract belief that God has given the land to Israel, a frequent refrain in Deuteronomy, also translates into resentment among the nonelite over the fact that land is very unevenly distributed and the tax burden falls disproportionately on them. The little tradition is not merely a passive receptacle for the great tradition, but injects its own interests and reconfigures the great tradition in accordance with the basic needs of survival.

The great tradition, however, is also often able to "mystify" certain aspects of itself such that the peasant is convinced that only the elite have certain key powers or access to the divine. Pilgrimage illustrates this dynamic, for the nonelite must travel to a holy site controlled by elites (Jerusalem for Judeans; Mecca for Muslims; Delphi or Dodona for Greeks; Prayaga [Allahabad] or Varanasi for Hindus). Priests, too, are accorded special powers of access: the Judean high priest alone was able to make atonement on Yom Kippur; in India, Brahmins, who are at the top of the caste system, have the exclusive right to perform certain rituals.

Yet the elites do not hold all of the power. While the elite may believe that they rule by divine right and consider the benefactions they give to the nonelite as their privilege to provide or to withhold, the nonelite often have a different view. The benefactions of the elite are often thought of as the *rights* of the nonelite. Nonperformance of the elite's obligations toward the nonelite can, therefore, lead to tension and resistance. Nonelite may devise ways to resist the extractions of elite by foot-dragging, tampering with weights and measures, hiding produce, and underpayment of taxes. A scene from the 1978 Italian movie *L'Albero degli zoccoli* (*The Tree of the Wooden Clogs*) shows tenant farmers loading their grain wagon with stones to increase its weight so that they would appear to pay the full amount of the rent to their landlord. In extreme circumstances, more drastic measures might be taken. Josephus reports that one of the first actions of the First Revolt was the destruction of debt archives in Jerusalem, an indication that high debt burdens were one of the causes of the revolt.[20] Thus, although the little tradition is dependent on the great tradition, it is also in tension with the perspective of the elite. Scott describes the little tradition as "a 'shadow society'—a pattern of structural, stylistic, and normative opposition to the politico-religious tradition of ruling elites."[21]

I have suggested earlier in this chapter that unlike the audiences presupposed by Matthew and Luke, and unlike those of the letters of Paul, the Jesus movement reflected in Q was a rural phenomenon. Q is replete with agricultural and rural metaphors: unproductive olive or fig trees being uprooted and burned (3:9); threshing and collecting wheat and burning the chaff (3:17); the requisitioning of laborers or farm animals by the military (Q/Matt. 5:41); the practice of measuring back agricultural loans by the same scoop used to make the loan (6:38); arboriculture (6:43–44); housebuilding in *wadis* where flash floods can destroy the house (6:47–49); day laborers employed for the harvest (10:2); the payment of day laborers (10:7); sowing and harvesting (12:24); burning grass in a furnace (12:28); litigants traveling *to the town* for court (12:58–59); the rapid growth of mustard (13:18–19; 17:6); shepherding (15:4–7); and field work (17:34).

For such a constituency we should expect that the religion of Israel was expressed concretely and oriented to the demands of daily life: subsistence, reproduction, managing relations at the village level, and defending villagers against the predations of the outside (taxes, rents, debt). Q indeed exemplifies just such concerns.

Subsistence and Debt

The Lord's Prayer, found in Q (11:2–4), has three petitions after the introduction:

> Give us our daily bread today;
> and cancel our debts for us, as we too have cancelled for those
>   in debt to us;
> and do not put us to the test!

The Greek term that is rendered "daily" is an exceedingly rare word, *epiousios*. In fact, this is the first occurrence of the word in all of Greek literature and for this reason it is not clear what it means. The best guess, offered first by Origen, is that it means "necessary for existence" (*epi* [for] + *ousia* [existence]). If this is so, the first petition concerns subsistence and reflects the belief that agricultural productivity—good seed, adequate rains, good harvests—are connected to God's beneficence. As Arthur Stinchcombe quipped, "Agriculture is always the kind of enterprise with which God has a lot to do."[22] The ability of the nonelite to feed themselves, however, is *also* a function of their ability to resist the extractions of landlords and tax gatherers.

Landlords knew this. Hence, contemporary leases and loan documents from Egypt are insistent in attaching penalties to the lessees and debtors for nonperformance of their duties. These agreements typically require that loans and lease payments be made with first-quality, clean, unadulterated, and sifted grain, "pressed down and leveled." Obviously, it was in the small producers' interests to repay loans and rents with less than top-quality grain and to contaminate the grain with heavy substances. Because loans, rents, and taxes were a zero-sum game, the more the elite could extract, the less was left for the peasant producer. The request to "give us our daily bread today" was thus a request that God underwrite the interests of the nonelite against the rich.

The second petition is equally focused on the daily realities of the nonelite. Although later users of the prayer have tended to metaphorize the term "debt," we should resist this temptation. In agrarian societies, debt is an endemic problem. The indebtedness of smallholders typically results in their loss of land and the transformation of the economy into a system of tenant farmers and nonslave laborers (*ergatai*), underemployed throughout most of the agricultural year.[23] Tenancy itself was not a remedy for debt, since rents usually skimmed off between one-half and two-thirds of the produce, leaving the tenant at or just below the subsistence level. One bad harvest could drive the tenant into debt from which he could not escape. If the landlord decided to reduce the rent, this act created an enduring obligation on the part of the tenant which could never be repaid.

The Q prayer proposes a quid pro quo: God will cancel their debts if the Q folk cancel each other's debts. This resembles the Qumran covenanters' rules for the sabbatical year:

> [Every creditor] who [has lent something to] someone, or [who possesses something from his brother] will grant a re[lease to his fell]ow for [God] your [God has proclaimed the release. You are to demand restitution] from the fore[igner, but from your brother] you shall not demand restitution, *for in that year [God will bless you, forgiving your] sins*. (1QWords of Moses 3.5–7)

God's release of sins is thus coordinated with the people's willingness to cancel debts. That Q really means "debt" and not some metaphorical equivalent is underscored by Q 6:30:

To the one who asks of you, give; and [[from the one who borrows, do not [[ask]] back [[«what is»]] yours.

Q thus proposes a social praxis in which indebtedness is replaced by a general reciprocity. Did Q try to influence those in a position to make loans to engage in this unusual practice? We cannot tell. But it is clear that Q mounts the argument that to do so qualifies one as morally superior to the ordinary exploitive practices of the elite:

³¹And the way you want people to treat you, that is how you treat them. ³²If you love those loving you, what reward do you have? Do not even tax collectors do the same? ³⁴And if you [[lend «to those» from whom you hope to receive, what <reward do> you <have>]]? Do not even [[the Gentiles]] do the same? (Q 6:31, 32, 34)

Notice that the measure-for-measure saying is framed to appeal to lenders:

[[And]] with the measure (*metron*) you use to measure out, it will be measured back to you. (6:38)

In ancient economic practice, the one who "measured out" and to whom it was "measured back" was the lender, not the borrower. The lender insisted that grain be returned using the same measuring scoop (*metron*) so that he or she could be guaranteed that the loan was repaid in full.²⁴ In the context of Q 6:36–38 and its injunction to "be merciful," the measure-for-measure saying serves to encourage *lenders* to engage in generous lending practice, invoking their own principle of repayment: if you lend generously, you will likewise be treated generously.

Yet Q is also acutely aware of the dangers of debt, of being dragged into court:

> [58][[While]] you «go along» with your opponent on the way, make an effort to get loose from him, lest [[the opponent]] hand you over to the judge, and the judge to the assistant, and [[the <assistant>]] throw [[you]] into prison. [59]I say to you: You will not get out of there until you pay the last *[[quadran]]*. (Q 12:58–59)

The last sentence indicates the context: the litigation is over money owed, probably loan or rental payments. It also worth observing that from Q's perspective, the opponent will win the case. The possibility that the debtor might be exonerated is not even entertained. This pessimism about the legal system is typical of the experience of nonelite, who know that judges (from the cities, of course) will rule in favor of their peers rather than in favor of the poorly dressed, filthy, and illiterate villager. Oakman adds that the final petition of Q's Lord's Prayer, "do not put us to the test," should also be seen in the context of worries about the consequences of being dragged into court in just the way that Q 12:58–59 imagines. Thus Q 11:4 is a kind of summary of the earlier petitions: "It is a vivid request for deliverance from hunger, debt, and trials in rigged courts before evil judges."[25]

Taxes

Oakman has also argued that many of Q's sayings disguise a discourse about taxes. The admonition to be "merciful" as God is merciful (Q 6:36), elaborated as "do not pass judgment, «so» you are not judged" (Q 6:37) is an admonition to stewards and tax collectors "not to execute against debtors."[26] Oakman also suggests that Q deliberately invokes language associated with tax collection, but inverts it in order to depict an alternate practice. The Q missionaries in Q 10:5–6 are to "enter" (*eiserchomai*) a house—the same verb used to describe the forced entry of a tax collector; but they enter with a greeting of peace and with healing. The statement

Are not [[five]] sparrows sold for [[two]] *assaria*? And yet not one of them will fall to earth without [[your Father's]] «consent» (Q 16:6–7)

is an ironic allusion of the fact that nothing was sold in the marketplace without the knowledge of tax collectors. But Q insists that it is ultimately God who surveils village life.

Storehouse economies are lampooned in Q 12:16–20, the story of the fool who builds bigger barns and then dies, and in Q 12:24. The elite (and the Romans) collect produce in storehouses. Yet,

> consider the ravens: They neither sow nor reap nor gather into barns (*apothekai*), and yet God feeds them. Are you not better than the birds? (Q 12:24)

This saying, according to Oakman, contains a pun. "Birds," in Hebrew *ṣippôrîm*, is related to the name Sepphoris, one of the main locations of storehouses and debt archives. The *Ṣippôrîm*, accordingly, are the people of Sepphoris. The saying contrasts those who cannot achieve the kind of surpluses that permit storage with those who can. But in God's view those who cannot accumulate surpluses are the ones favored by God. A similar pun may be present in Q 9:58, "Foxes have holes, and birds of the sky have nests; but the son of man does not have anywhere he can lay his head." The contrast is between "the life of the elites at Sepphoris . . . with their extensive storehouses" and the lifestyle of the Son of Man.[27]

Although it is precarious to build too much on possible puns and instances of double entrendre, especially when it requires a retro-translation of Q's Greek into Aramaic or Hebrew, at the same time it is typical of nonelite-elite relationships that the nonelite will speak in a kind of double-speak, at one level appearing to communicate directly with outsiders, but using the same language to encode alternate views of reality that resist the elite, making fun of their names and practices, and justifying acts of resistance. Oakman's suggestions on Q 12:24 and 9:58 would be excellent instances of nonelite language that lampoons the elite.

Local Solidarity

Recently Melanie Johnson-Debaufre has made a convincing case that Q is less interested in erecting walls between insiders to the Jesus movement and outsiders based on their recognition of Jesus. Instead, Q endeavors to persuade fellow Judeans to recognize their common cause. Q 11:19–20 is a case in point:

> [19]And if I by Beelzebul cast out demons, your sons, by whom do they cast «them» out? This is why they will be your judges. [20]But if it is by the finger of God that I cast out demons, then there has come upon you God's reign.

Many commentators see a tension between Q 11:19, which appears to recognize God's hand in the activities of contemporary exorcists, and Q 11:20, which appears to claim exclusive mediation of the kingdom for Jesus. For Johnson-DeBaufre, however, there is no tension. Following Tertullian, she argues that 11:19–20 makes a case for solidarity:

> [T]he *basileia* [reign] of God is the common ground on which the text calls all Jews to stand against the *basileia* of Satan. The text appeals to the audience to avoid the divisiveness inherent in the claim that Jesus is not on the right side. This suggests that the Q community told this controversy story not to assert the singularity of Jesus or the superiority of their Jewishness but rather to make the case for the communal vision of the *basileia* of God over against the *basileia* of Satan.[28]

Likewise, Johnson-DeBaufre proposes that for Q 7:31–35, Q places Jesus and John on the same side, despite their obviously different lifestyles:

> [33]For John came, neither eating nor drinking, and you say: He has a demon! [34]The son of man came, eating and drinking, and you say: Look! A person «who is» a glutton and

drunkard, a friend of tax collectors and sinners! [35]But Wisdom was vindicated by her children.

She insists that Q's comparison of "this generation" with querulous children (Q 7:32) is not designed to draw sharp lines between Jesus/John and "this generation," but rather to appeal to "this generation" to abandon divisive and factional behavior and to recognize their common ground.[29] On this view, then, Christology (the theological characterization of Jesus) is less important than creating solidarity among Judeans. Needless to say, with the absorption of Q into Matthew and Luke, both of whom had a strong christological interest, this perspective was lost from view.

Inversionary Language in Q

We also find instances of deliberate inversions in Q. Take the first makarism in Q:

> Blessed are [[«you»]] poor, for God's reign is for [[you]].
> (Q 6:20b)

"Blessed" (*makarios*) in Greek is normally associated with the gods, with the dead, or with the upper strata of society, who are "blessed" with wealth, privilege, high birth, influence, and honor and who do not suffer the ordinary depredations of life. In the Hebrew Bible the blessed are those who attend the king (1 Kgs. 10:18; 2 Chr. 9:7), who *consider* the poor (but are not poor themselves!) (Ps. 41:1), and priests who dwell in the temple (Ps. 84:4).

> Blessedness is fulness of life; it relates first to earthly blessings, a wife (Sir. 25:8; 26:1), children (Gn. 30:13; 4 Macc. 16:9; 18:9; Ps. 126:5; Sir. 25:7), beauty (Cant. 6:9 [8]), earthly well-being, riches, honor, wisdom (Job 29:10, 11, cf. also Is. 32:20).[30]

By contrast Q pronounces the *ptochoi*, the ultra-poor, blessed. Whether this embodies an expectation about how things will be

in the near future, when God intervenes, or whether it is a statement about the current order of things, the makarism implies an
inversion of the elite way of looking at things. Other sayings in Q
support this view: the story in Q 12:16–20 of a rich man who wants
to build bigger and bigger storehouses, but dies that night, lampoons the elite notion of blessedness, and admonishes. Q
11:16–34 concludes,

> «Do not treasure for yourselves treasures on earth, where
> moth and gnawing deface and where robbers dig through
> and rob,» but treasure for yourselves treasure«s» in heaven,
> where neither moth nor gnawing defaces and where robbers
> do not dig through nor rob. For where your treasure is, there
> will also be your heart. (Q 12:33–34)

Q 12:33–34 focuses on the hoarding activities of the elite, pointing out that wealth is ephemeral and subject to decay. Ultimately
Q claims that the pursuit of wealth is inimical to devotion to God:

> No one can serve two masters; for a person will either hate the
> one and love the other, or be devoted to the one and despise
> the other. You cannot serve God and mammon. (Q 16:13)

These examples—which could be multiplied—should be sufficient to make the point that for Q, religion has to do with the
basics of life: subsistence, debt, communal relationships, and
interaction with those outside the village. Some of its admonitions
are aimed at villagers and others at creditors and landlords who
might be influenced by a vision of God's reign, in which attachment to wealth, the storage of surpluses, and debt-extraction are
not practiced. In their place, Q looks forward to the practice of
general reciprocity. The reign of God, to adapt and invert Paul in
Romans 14:17, consisted precisely in food and drink, in debt
relief, and in mercy and justice.

This utopian vision was eventually effaced by the editing of
Matthew and Luke. Matthew moralized much of Q, so that Q's
"blessed are you poor" became "blessed are the *poor in spirit*," a

declaration of the blessedness of the meek. Luke did not moralize Q in this way, but where Q advocated general reciprocity, Luke would enjoin the rich to be benefactors of the poor. The poor again become objects of the largesse of the rich.

A Different Gospel

The center of Q's teachings is not, as it is in Mark, the identity of Jesus as the son of God, but rather the behavior and attitudes that reflect God's reign. There is, of course, some interest in the identity of Jesus, who is called the One to Come and the Son of Man. But much more space is devoted to articulating the *ethos* of the reign of God. Sophia, God's wisdom, is the supervening force in Q's world; the kingdom of God is more important than the death and resurrection of Jesus. Jesus is not a suffering messiah who dies as expiation for sins but, as Burton Mack puts it, "a sage whose sayings and the wisdom to be derived from them made all the difference that mattered."[31] The Q folk, to be sure, looked to Jesus as the privileged teacher who, above all others, was the model for emulation. There is not much evidence that this Jesus was memorialized as a savior, as he was in the Christ-confessing churches of Paul. As Crossan puts it, the continuity between Jesus and the Q folk "is not in mnemonics but in mimetics, not in remembrance but in imitation, not in word but in deed."[32]

Thus, the Sayings Gospel Q represents a *different gospel*. It is a gospel that circulated not among urbanites, but among the rural poor, not in the Gentile cities of the east, but in the towns of Jewish Galilee. It took significantly different views of miracles, Jesus' death, and Jesus' vindication than what is found in the Synoptics and Paul. Its ethical teachings give us a glimpse of the life and attitudes, not of the urban classes in which the Jesus movement eventually spread, but the villages and towns of the Galilee, where God's actions and reign had everything to do with the basics of life: food, debt, the supports for ordinary life and the threats to it.

Chapter Four

Q, *Thomas*, and James

What happened to Q? Why did it disappear? The simplest answer is that we simply don't know. Plenty of other early Christian documents disappeared along with Q. The letter Paul first wrote to the Corinthians (1 Cor. 5:9) was not preserved. The letter mentioned in Colossians 4:16 has likewise gone missing. We also have the names of several Jewish Christian Gospels that have disappeared except for a handful of excerpts quoted by early church authors: the *Gospel of the Ebionites*, the *Gospel of the Hebrews*, the *Gospel of the Egyptians*. Papyrus scraps of other documents are known—*Papyrus Egerton 2*, *Papyrus Oxyrhynchus* 840, *Papyrus Oxyrhynchus* 1224, and the *Gospel of Peter*—but the full copies of these are lost.

Some scholars have attempted to offer explanations of Q's disappearance. One of the first suggestions was by the British scholar G. D. Kilpatrick, who surmised that if Q had been almost completely copied by Matthew and Luke, its disappearance might have a simple explanation: absorbed into more complex and elaborate documents, there was no reason to keep Q.[1] This is surely possible. The obvious objection, of course, is that the same ought then to have happened with Mark, since more than 90 percent of Mark was copied by either Matthew or Luke or both. Kilpatrick's explanation cannot be a sufficient explanation.

Other scholars propose that Q's disappearance had to do with questionable contents or with the perception that it was somehow theologically deficient. James Dunn, for example, speculated that the reason for Q's ultimate disappearance was that it was "not treated as gospel by most of the early Christians" and was perhaps even regarded as too amenable to gnosticizing distortions.[2] Neither of these explanations is particularly convincing, however. All that we can safely surmise is that Matthew and Luke treated Q as an authoritative source, just as they did with Mark. In fact as I have noted earlier, Matthew and Luke preserved Q's wording *better* on average than they preserved the wording of Mark. We have no way to gauge how other early Christians regarded Q. Hence, we simply don't know whether they treated it as a gospel or not.

If Dunn's point is that Q, when compared with Matthew and Luke, does not have as complex a set of theological concepts, the point may be granted. But if theological complexity were the criterion for preservation, we would be hard pressed to account for the preservation of documents such as the letter of James or the *Didache*, both of which are largely didactic and neither of which has a complex theology. For that matter, the preservation of Paul's letter to Philemon cannot have been due to its theological contents. It is essentially a private letter of Paul to Philemon on a matter concerning a slave. Other reasons will have to be proposed for the preservation or nonpreservation of early Christian materials.

As to Q's supposed proclivity to "gnosticizing distortions," there is no evidence of this at all. What Dunn apparently had in mind is a suggestion made long ago by James Robinson. Robinson argued that as a sayings collection featuring the figure of the "Heavenly Sophia" (Q 7:35; 11:49–51; 13:34–35?), Q belonged to a trajectory of wisdom books that began with Proverbs and ended in gnostic dialogues.[3] The tendency immanent in this genre was to associate the speaker of wise words with Heavenly Sophia herself, and eventually to transform the speaker into a gnostic redeemer figure. A careful examination of Near Eastern wisdom collections indicates, however, that there is no necessary or inevitable "gnosticizing tendency" operative in wisdom collections.[4] Neither the Mishnah's

'*Abot*, a collection of the sayings of early rabbinic sages, nor the *Sentences of Sextus*, a Christian collection of wise sayings, shows any gnosticizing proclivity, as Robinson himself later recognized.[5] Indeed, Q itself has nothing that could reasonably be termed "gnostic"—that is, a tendency toward an antimaterial dualism, or the claim that the human soul is a spark of the divine now imprisoned in the world, or that the redeemer's role is to awaken sleeping sparks of life and thus to bring about a reunification of the divine.

Dunn's theological explanation seems to be an ad hoc response to Q, for surely he would not explain the disappearance of the lost Pauline letter to the Corinthians (1 Cor. 5:9) or the deutero-Pauline letter to the Laodiceans (Col. 4:16) by suggesting that they were not copied because they were heterodox or inadequate. Dunn's proposal in fact assumes a level of theological analysis and surveillance in the early Jesus movement which cannot be demonstrated to have existed. We have no reason to suppose that early copyists subjected their documents to an orthodoxy test. Indeed, it is anachronistic to speak of "orthodoxy" in the first century CE. Rather than preservation on the basis of a narrowly defined orthodoxy, it is more likely that one of the key ingredients in preservation of documents had to do with the ascription of those documents to distinguished personage—Paul, any of the apostles, John of Patmos, Mark, Luke, James, Jude, Barnabas, Polycarp (whether or not these attributions were correct). Of course, even this did not help in the case of Paul's lost letter to the Corinthians.

A better explanation of the disappearance of Q is offered by Dieter Lührmann. The preservation and disappearance of documents was largely a matter of chance, he says. Before the fourth century,

> the circumstances of the transmission of the Jesus tradition are so haphazard that Q would have had to be known in Egypt for us to possess a fragment of it. Even for the Gospel of Mark . . . there is only a single manuscript [from Egypt, namely $\mathfrak{P}^{45}$—the Chester Beatty I papyrus, from the mid-

third century CE], and that derives from circles which already accepted the canon of Irenaeus.[6]

Q may have disappeared simply because it was not adopted by one of the communities or groups of communities of the second and third centuries with the resources to recopy documents and distribute them in their networks. Or Q's disappearance may have been an accident of geography: Q was never copied in Egypt and thus perished along with other documents whose manuscripts could not survive the more humid climates of other parts of the Mediterranean. Or it may have been an accident of history: Q was used by Galilean or Palestinian groups which did not survive the First Revolt, or which simply died out. Theologians sometimes suffer from the conceit that everything connected with Christianity occurred for a theological reason. But this is rarely the way in which history works. The details of history are full of random events and accidents that dramatically change its course.

Sayings of Jesus in the Early Church

Perhaps Q did not disappear entirely. Or at least Q-like collections did not disappear entirely. Clement of Rome, writing about 95 CE, admonishes his addressees to be humble, laying aside arrogance, conceit, folly, and anger, and buttresses this with a quotation which resembles Q 6:36–38:

> For thus [Jesus] said, Be merciful, that you may receive mercy; forgive, that you may be forgiven; as you do, so shall it be done to you. As you give, so shall it be given unto you. As you judge, so shall you be judged. As you show kindness, so shall kindness be showed to you. With the measure that you measure out, with the same measure it will be measured back to you. (*1 Clem.* 13:2)

[36]Be merciful, just as your Father is merciful. [37]Do not pass judgment, «so» you are not judged. [[For with what judgment you pass judgment, you will be judged.]] [38][[And]] with

the measure you use to measure out, it will be measured back
to you. (Q 6:36–38)

Clement's citation is much more elaborate than that found in Q,
consisting of six stylized imperatives and a buttressing maxim. The
key difference between Clement's version and Q is that Q *prohibits*
judgment while Clement only limits it. It might be thought that
the combination of the admonition to be merciful (Q 6:36) and an
imperative about judging (Q 6:37) with the measure-for-measure
saying (Q 6:38) would suggest that *1 Clement* 13.2 is ultimately
dependent upon Q. Mark knows the measure-for-measure saying
(Mark 4:24) but uses it in a completely different context, uncon-
nected to admonitions to show mercy or judgment. The case for
dependence would be much stronger if *1 Clement* had a greater
density of allusions to the Jesus tradition. Since *1 Clement* 13.2 and
46.8 are the only such allusions, it seems precarious to posit knowledge of Q. Andrew Gregory concludes:

> The stylized form of [Clement's] maxims gives them an iden-
> tity apart from the Synoptic Gospels, and their rhythmic
> structure together with the introductory formula might be
> taken to suggest an oral rather than a written source. What-
> ever its possible relationship to Q, this citation is evidence to
> support the hypothesis that there were collections of sayings
> of Jesus other than but not dissimilar to those found in the
> Synoptic Gospels.[7]

The only other possible allusion to Q in *1 Clement* comes in his
invective against factionalism:

> Remember the words of Jesus our Lord, for he said: Woe to
> that man; it would be better had he not been born, rather
> than that at he should offend one of my elect. It would be
> better for him that a millstone were hanged about him and
> be cast into the sea, than that he should pervert one of my
> elect. (*1 Clem.* 46.8)

¹It is necessary for offenses to come, but woe «to the one»
through whom they come! ²It is better for him [[if]] a millstone is put around his neck and he is thrown into the sea,
than that he should offend one of these little ones. (Q 17:1–2)

Again Clement's version is more complex, incorporating a woe
that also appears in Mark 14:21 (said of Judas), "woe to that
man . . . it would be better had that man not been born." Since *1
Clement*'s version incorporates nothing that is distinctive in Q's
version—for example, its association with other admonitions on
forgiveness or faith (17:3–4, 6)—it is impossible to distinguish
between Clement's use of Q and his use of a free-floating woe.

Some of the sayings that appear in Q appear in other contexts as
well. The *Didache* or "Teachings of the Twelve Apostles," written
sometime in the first century and supplemented in the early to mid-
second century CE, contains some sayings that also appear in Q:

> Let every apostle who comes to you be received as the Lord.
>   (*Did*. 11.4)
> Let everyone who comes to you in the name of the Lord
>   be received, and then examining him you shall know,
>   for you will have understanding of what is true and false.
>   (*Did*. 12:1)
> Whoever receives you receives me, [[and]] whoever receives
>   me receives the one who sent me. (Q 10:16)

Both of the *Didache's* statements imply that traveling envoys ought
to be welcomed. The obvious difference between Q's formulation
and the *Didache's* is that the latter is framed from the point of view
of the group that is to *receive* envoys, while Q's saying serves to jus-
tify the activities of the envoys themselves. While there is some
general conceptual similarity, it would be difficult to make a case
that the *Didache* knew Q, since the *Didache* does not betray the
slightest knowledge of any of the context that Q gives to this saying (Q 10:2–16). The *Didache* may have used a floating maxim that
also found its way into Q. In any event, the *Didache* has elaborated

the maxim in 12.1 by adding the injunction to *testing* visiting apostles, a development unattested in Q.

A more distant echo of a Q saying is found in *Didache* 11.7 and *Gospel of Thomas* 44:

> Do not test or examine any prophet who is speaking in the spirit; for every sin will be forgiven, but this sin will not be forgiven. (*Did*. 11.7)

> And whoever says a word against the son of man, it will be forgiven him; but whoever [[speaks]] against the holy Spirit, it will not be forgiven him. (Q 12:10)

> Jesus says: Whoever blasphemes against the father, it will be forgiven him. And whoever blasphemes against the son, it will be forgiven him. But whoever blasphemes against the holy spirit, it will not be forgiven him, neither on earth nor in heaven. (*Gos. Thom*. 44)

As the *Didache*'s saying makes clear, the warning about the unforgivable sin is used in relation to the testing of prophets while they are speaking in a trance. Q's warning, by contrast, appears in an entirely difference context, in a warning against denying Jesus in the midst of persecution. The *Gospel of Thomas*'s saying is much closer to Q's version, relegating blasphemy of Jesus to a lesser grade of seriousness than blasphemy of the spirit. The *Didache*'s version looks like an attenuated version of the longer Q/Thomas maxim, but applied quite differently.

The *Didache* explains that a prophet or teacher who wishes to settle in a community should be supported, justifying this with a maxim similar to one found in Q's mission speech:

> ¹But every true prophet who wishes to settle among you is worthy of his food (*trophē*). ²Likewise a true teacher is himself worthy, like the laborer [*ergatēs*], of his food [*trophē*]. (*Did*. 13.1–2)

⁷[[And at that house]] remain, «eating and drinking whatever they provide», for the day laborer [*ergates*] is worthy of his wages [*misthoi*]. (Q 10:7)

For the scripture says, "You shall not muzzle an ox while it is treading out the grain," and, "The laborer is worthy of his wages" [*misthoi*]. (1 Tim. 5:18)

The *Didache*'s formulation is closer to Matthew's version, which also uses "food" (*trophē*, Matt. 10:10) rather than "wages" (Q 10:7). The difference is not incidental, for the Matthew/*Didache* version presupposes the practice of feeding the workers attached to a household, who typically received upkeep (cf. Q 12:42) rather than wages. Q uses the metaphor of God sending out workers *hired daily* to perform the harvesting (Q 10:2, 7b), a standard practice in estate agriculture.⁸ Such workers naturally received wages. Thus, the "workers" of Matthew/*Didache* represent a higher and more secure class of workers, attached to a household that undertook to feed them, while Q's workers are like the workers of Matthew 20:1–14, hired daily if they are lucky. It would be difficult to establish a direct connection between the *Didache* and Q. It is noteworthy, however, that the *Didache*, like Q, refers to the traveling envoy or teacher as an *ergates*, a laborer, which would not be a usual title of respect. In the second century, 1 Timothy also uses this term to refer to community leaders. The pastoral writer's erroneous impression that the saying is scriptural—only his first citation, "you shall not muzzle an ox while it is treading grain," is from Deuteronomy 25:4—probably implies that the saying was commonly used in early Christian circles (and hence *assumed* to be scriptural). If this is so, it is even more difficult to conclude that the *Didache* can only derive from Q.

The closest parallels to Q preserved by the *Didache* are found in *Didache* 1.3–5, universally regarded as an insertion into the *Didache*'s Two Ways section (*Did.* 1.1–6.1):

³Now, the teaching of these words is this: Bless those that curse you, and pray for your enemies, and fast for those that

persecute you. For what credit is it to you if you love those that love you? Do not even the Gentiles do the same? But, for your part, love those that hate you, and you will have no enemy. [4]Abstain from fleshly and bodily desires. If any one strikes you on the right cheek, turn to him the other cheek also, and thou will be perfect. If any man requisition thee to go with him one mile, go with him two. If any man take your cloak, give him your tunic also. If anyone will take from you what is yours, refuse it not—not even if thou can [or: for you cannot].

[5]Give to everyone that asks you, and do not refuse, for the Father's will is that we give to all from the gifts we have received. Blessed is he that gives according to the mandate; for he is innocent. Woe to him who receives; for if any man receive alms under pressure of need he is innocent; but he who receives it without need shall be tried as to why he took and for what, and being in prison he shall be examined as to his deeds, and he shall not come out thence until he pay the last *quadran*.

The similarities of this to Q 6:27–28, 32–34; Q/Matt. 5:41; Q 6:29–30; and Q 12:58–59 are striking. Yet analysis of this catena of sayings in the *Didache* indicates that whoever inserted this cluster of sayings into the *Didache* knew the *Lukan* version of some of the sayings. Whether the author also knew Matthew or Q is impossible to determine, since at the points where the *Didache* agrees with Matthew, Matthew is copying Q with few changes.[9] Hence, it is not clear that the *Didache* is a witness to Q, though that possibility cannot be excluded entirely.

The Gospel of Thomas *and Q*

Three Greek fragments containing lists of sayings of Jesus prefaced by "Jesus said" were discovered among the Oxyrhynchus papyri in the 1890s in Upper Egypt. For the first part of the twentieth century these three fragments, *Papyrus Oxyrhynchus* I 1; IV 654, 655, were known as the *Logia Iēsou*. The two papyrologists who published the fragments immediately saw their connection to Q, although they did not claim that the Oxyrhynchus fragments came from Q:

> In any case we may have got for the first time a concrete example of what was meant by the Logia which Papias tells us were compiled by St. Matthew, and the *logia kyriaka* [the Lord's Logia] upon which Papias himself wrote a commentary.[10]

With the discovery of a full Coptic version of the *Gospel of Thomas* in 1945, it became clear that the three Oxyrhynchus fragments were earlier Greek copies of the *Gospel of Thomas*. The discovery of a "gospel" that consisted exclusively of sayings, without any reference to the death and resurrection, was sensational, and initiated a fresh examination of Q. No longer was it necessary to imagine that Q was a supplement of the passion *kerygma*. Q could well represent a discrete and autonomous type of early Christian theologizing, and ultimately be a gospel in its own right.[11]

Thomas presents sayings of Jesus *seriatim*, introduced simply by "Jesus says" or occasionally, "The disciples said." Take for example sayings 25–26:

> 25 Jesus says: Love your brother like your life! Protect him like the apple of your eye!
> 26 Jesus says: You see the splinter that is in your brother's eye, but you do not see the beam that is in your (own) eye. When you remove the beam from your eye, then you will see clearly (enough) to remove the splinter in your brother's eye.

The first *Thomas* saying appears to be a variant of Leviticus 19:18, "you shall love your neighbor as yourself," or the *Didache*'s "you shall not hate anyone . . . and some you shall love more than your own soul" (2.7). The second *Thomas* saying finds a parallel in Q 6:43–44. The two sayings appear to be joined on the basis of the *catchwords*, "your brother" and "eye." This is a composition technique also found in wisdom books such as Proverbs.

Other kinds of linkages are attested. Some clusters of sayings are joined by common formulae or common forms. Sayings 96–98 all begin "The kingdom of the father is like . . ." and then tell a parable. In other instances a common theme unifies the sayings. Sayings 63–65, consisting also of three parables, are all about wealthy persons whose pursuit of wealth obscures more important pursuits.[12]

Q displays many of the same associative techniques. Some sayings are connected by catchwords, famously Q 12:33–34 and Q 12:39–40, connected on the basis of two catchwords, "dig through" and "robber":

> [33]«Do not treasure for yourselves treasures on earth, where moth and gnawing deface and where robbers (*kleptai*) dig through (*diorussein*) and rob,» but treasure for yourselves treasure«s» in heaven, where neither moth nor gnawing defaces and where robbers (*kleptai*) do not dig through (*diorussein*) nor rob. [34]For where your treasure is, there will also be your heart.

> [39]But know [[this]]: If the householder had known in which watch the robber (*kleptēs*) was coming, he would not have let his house be dug into (*diorussein*). [40]You also must be ready, for the Son of man is coming at an hour you do not expect.

The irony of this association is that in the first saying the point is to obtain possessions that cannot *in principle* be stolen, while in the second saying the household prevents the theft of things that can be stolen. But then Q adds another saying that implicitly compares the Son of Man to a robber who cannot be stopped! The use of catchword association often creates pairs of sayings that do not quite fit conceptually, as is the case here.

Some of Q's sayings are joined together on the basis of formal similarity: four sayings beginning with "blessed are . . ." (Q 6:20–23), seven sayings all beginning "woe . . ." (Q 11:39–52), and two double parables at Q 13:18–19 || 20–21; 15:4–7 || 8–10) and several double sayings (11:31 || 32; 12:24 || 27; 17:26–27 || 28–30; 17:34 || 35). Still others are joined on the basis of thematic associations such as the mention of John the Baptist (Q 7:18–23,

24–27, 28, 29–30, 31–35) or disputes with Jesus' opponents (Q 11:14–23, 24–26, 29–32).

On balance, Q achieves a greater degree of internal organization than *Thomas*. As noted in chapter 3, the editors of Q have created relatively extended discursive settings, for example, the initial speech to disciples (Q 6:20–49), or sayings on mission and prayer (Q 9:57–62; 10:2–16; 21–22; 23–24; 11:2–4, 9–13). *Thomas* is rarely able to connect more than two or three sayings, but Q, through its editorial techniques, is able to imply that a dozen or more sayings were spoken on the same occasion. Nevertheless, both Q and the *Gospel of Thomas* fall squarely within the range of organizational features attested in other ancient sayings collections.[13]

If there is a *generic* relationship between Q and the *Gospel of Thomas* is there a *genetic* relationship as well? *Thomas* shares with Q 37 or almost one-third of its 114 sayings (although sometimes *Thomas* has two or three parallels to Q in the same saying).[14] Of Q's 92 units,[15] there are 42 contacts with *Thomas* (again, sometimes one Q saying has several different resonances with *Thomas*). The overlap between Q and *Thomas* is substantial, far more than the overlap between Q and *1 Clement* or Q and the *Didache*. Despite this, it is almost impossible to propose a scenario whereby either *Thomas* drew on Q or Q drew on *Thomas*.

Thomas shares with Q many aphorisms, including saying 47:

> [1]Jesus says: It is impossible for a person to mount two horses and to stretch two bows. [2]And it is impossible for a servant to serve two masters. Or he will honor [*timan*] the one and insult [*hybrizein*] the other. [3]No person drinks old wine and immediately desires to drink new wine. [4]And new wine is not put into old wineskins, so that they do not burst; nor is old wine put into (a) new wineskin, so that it does not spoil it. [5]An old patch is not sewn onto a new garment, because a tear will result. (*Gos. Thom.* 47.1–5)

> No one can serve two masters; for a person will either hate [*misein*] the one and love [*agapein*] the other, or be devoted [*anthexesthai*] to the one and despise [*kataphronein*] the other. You cannot serve God and Mammon. (Q 16:13)

As can be seen, Q's "serving two masters" saying has been applied to a theme that appears elsewhere, a criticism of attachment to wealth. *Thomas*'s saying, by contrast, is not only longer than Q's, with a triple illustration drawn from the worlds of equestrianism, archery, and household slavery, but is also connected with a series of other impossible or imprudent actions. Moreover, *Thomas* lacks Q's criticism of wealth, despite the fact that elsewhere *Thomas* criticizes commerce and wealth (*Gos. Thom.* 64). Note, too, that although the *sense* of the "serving two masters" saying is the same, the two versions have made entirely different choices in the pairs of verbs used. Since the two versions are developed in different directions and are articulated differently, it is difficult to conclude that either *Thomas* used Q or Q used *Thomas*.

Thomas also has parallels to several of Q's beatitudes:

Q 6:20a	Blessed are the poor	*Gos. Thom.* 54
Q 6:21	Blessed are the hungry	*Gos. Thom.* 69.2
Q 6:22–23	Blessed are the persecuted	*Gos. Thom.* 68; 69.1

Given the way that Thomas distributes the parallels to Q's beatitudes, it would be difficult to conclude that Thomas drew directly upon Q, for in that case Thomas would have broken up a coherent set of beatitudes for no apparent reason.

Or we might compare the *Gospel of Thomas* 21.5–7 with Q 12:34–40:

> [5]"That is why I say: When the master of the house learns that the thief is about to come, he will be on guard before he comes (and) will not let him break into his house, his domain, to carry away his possessions. [6](But) you, be on guard against the world! [7]Gird your loins with great strength, so that the robbers will not find a way to get to you. (*Gos. Thom.* 21.5–7)

> [39]But know [[this]]: If the householder had known in which watch the robber was coming, he would not have let his house be dug into. [40]You also must be ready, for the son of man is coming at an hour you do not expect. (Q 12:39–40)

Q employs the analogy of the householder guarding against a housebreaker in an odd way, to undergird the admonition to be ready for the coming of the Son of Man. As I have already noted, Q's example is one of a person *preventing* the coming of a thief by being ready; yet, the very next saying (v. 40) describes a situation that one *cannot* prevent by vigilance. In this respect, *Thomas*'s use of the analogy is much more natural: just as one can guard against a housebreaker, one can also guard against the intrusions of "the world." But *both* applications of this analogy appear to be secondary developments, Q in the direction of future eschatology, and *Thomas* in the direction of asceticism against the world. It would be very difficult to derive Q's application from *Thomas* or vice versa.

There is not enough space to consider each of *Thomas*'s overlaps with Q, but it is perhaps sufficient to quote Helmut Koester's conclusions:

> It can be said with confidence that the Q parallels in the Gospel of Thomas always represent, or derive from, more original forms of those sayings. Not only is there no trace of redactional features of Q in these sayings of the Gospel of Thomas, but they are also either core sayings of the respective sections of Q in which they occur or free sayings added at a later state of the development of Q.[16]

Koester's key point is that *Thomas* nowhere displays any knowledge of those elements in Q which are likely *editorial*: a criticism of "this generation," the use of Deuteronomistic theology, allusions to the fate of Sodom. *Thomas* famously lacks any of the Son of Man sayings that Q employs to describe the future role of the son of Man as a figure who will come suddenly with destruction and judgment (Q 12:8–9; 17:23–37). *Thomas*'s only Son of Man saying (86) has a parallel with Q 9:58, which describes the present state of the Son of Man as homeless.

Was James the Way Q Was Meant to Be Used?

1 Clement and the *Didache* used individual sayings which *also* found their way into Q. The *Gospel of Thomas* shares the same genre of sayings collection with Q, and perhaps originated in the same way, through a process of the aggregation of individual sayings of

Jesus into clusters organized by common catchword, common form, or common theme. Is there any other evidence of the direct use of Q, apart from Matthew and Luke's copying of Q into their Gospels?

For many years it has been recognized that the letter of James displays numerous conceptual parallels with the Jesus tradition, even though James never expressly attributes any of its contents to Jesus. Estimates vary about how many times James alludes to the Jesus tradition, but a good number to work with is that proposed by Patrick Hartin, who suggests twenty-six parallels.[17] What is remarkable is the density of allusions and the fact that almost all are sayings known from Q.[18]

Could James know Q? Hartin concludes that the density of parallels with Q texts (and the lack of parallels with Mark, John, or the non-Q portions of Matthew and Luke), suggest that this is the case:

> Only two possible explanations can be given of these simi-
> larities. Either both James and Q are dependent upon a com-
> mon tradition which is reflected in these examples; or James
> is dependent directly on the Q tradition. The argument of
> this investigation supports the direct dependence of James
> on Q. The main reason for opting for this second possibility
> arises from the closeness of the language used. While no one
> example is capable of proving the point conclusively, all these
> examples taken together provide an argument from conver-
> gence. If one were to opt for the first possibility whereby
> James and Q are independent of each other, yet dependent
> upon a common tradition, one would in fact have to postu-
> late a common tradition very similar to Q.[19]

As I have stressed throughout this chapter, this conclusion is justified only if James betrays knowledge of *editorial features* of Q, rather than simply sharing some of the same sayings with Q. In this case, however, we can point to places where James has taken over features of sayings that are likely due to Q's editing.[20]

James 1:5 is routinely seen as a parallel to Q 11:9–10:

⁵If someone lacks wisdom let him ask [*aiteitō*] it from the God who gives to all simply and without reproach, and it will be given to him [*kai dothēsetai autō*]. (James 1:5)

⁹I tell you, ask [*aiteite*] and it will be given to you [*kai dothēsetai hymin*], search and you will find, knock and it will be opened to you. ¹⁰For everyone who asks receives, and the one who searches finds, and to the one who knocks will it be opened. (Q 11:9–10)

The "searching and finding" aphorism is widely attested in the Jesus tradition, appearing in Q 11:9–10; James 1:5; *Papyrus Oxyrynchus* IV 654.6–9 (*Gospel of Thomas* 2), *Gospel of Thomas* 92, 94; *Gospel of Hebrews* 4a.b; *Dialogue of the Savior* 9–12, 20d; John 14:13–14; 15:7, 16b; 16:23–24, 26—twelve separate occurrences. In most of these performances, the principal verb pair is search-find rather than ask-give, and the sayings have to do with seeking *wisdom* or *life*. This application of the saying is appropriate of course, given the association in biblical wisdom literature between the verbs "seek" and "find" and wisdom or life.[21]

In the Sayings Gospel Q the search-find aphorism has been transformed and related to the practice of *prayer*. Q's aphorism was prefaced by the Lord's Prayer (Q 11:2–4), and then buttressed by the illustrations in Q 11:11–13 (unattested in any of the other occurrences of the admonition).

¹¹What person of you, whose son asks for *bread*, will *give* him a stone? ¹²Or again when he asks for a fish, will give him a snake? ¹³So if you, though evil, know how to give good gifts to your children, by how much more will the *Father* from heaven give good things to those who ask him! (Q 11:11–13)

These illustrations pick up and repeat the key vocabulary from the Lord's Prayer ("father," "bread," "give") and interpret "asking" as *praying* to the "Father from heaven." Q's interest in the aphorism is not in searching-finding or knocking-opening, but only in asking–being given. Thus, an aphorism that did not originally have *specifically* to do with prayer has been given a setting where "to ask" (*aitein*) now means "to pray."[22] Of the twelve occurrences of the admonition, only Q, James 1:5, and three occurrences in John employ the verb "ask" (*aitein*) with this connotation. The appearance in James of an editorial connection that was apparently first made by Q suggests strongly that James is not simply drawing on a saying that Q also used. James is drawing on Q itself.

Why should we not think that James knew Matthew or Luke? The answer is that while James shows affinities with Q sayings, James is ignorant of Matthew's editing of Q and Luke's editing of Q. Had James been using Matthew, we should expect him to take over features of Matthew's editing. For example, James alludes to the first beatitude in 2:5:

> Has God not chosen the poor as far as the world is concerned
> to be rich in faith and heirs of the kingdom that he promised
> to those who love him?

James betrays no knowledge of Matthew's distinctive way of referring to the kingdom as "the kingdom of the heavens" or his transformation of "poor" into "poor in spirit" (i.e., humble). Neither does James show knowledge of Lukan editing. Q concludes its argument about God's goodness in answering prayer with the statement,

> So if you, though evil, know how to give good gifts to your
> children, how much more will the Father from heaven give
> good things to those who ask him! (Q 11:13),

a statement that is perhaps echoed in James 1:17, "every good gift and perfect benefaction is from above, descending from the father of lights." But according to Luke, what God gives above all is the Holy Spirit, and he has altered Q 11:13 accordingly:

> If you then, who are evil, know how to give good gifts to your
> children, how much more will the heavenly Father give the
> *Holy Spirit* to those who ask him! (Luke 11:13)

James does not use the term "holy spirit" at all, and does not mention the spirit in connection with his argument about prayer. In other words, there is no evidence here, or elsewhere, that James is aware of specifically Matthean or Lukan developments of Q.

If it is the case that James knows Q, how can we account for two facts: that James never attributes any of the content of his teaching to Jesus, and that often James's formulations are close in meaning to Q, but not especially close in wording?

In order to answer both questions let's look at the ways in which ancient texts were employed. Of course, a text might be quoted verbatim and introduced as a quotation. This is the way Matthew quotes the Hebrew Bible (in its Greek translation). Texts could be copied, as Matthew and Luke have copied portions of Q almost verbatim. There was also a common technique that involved the *adaptation* of a predecessor text, especially if that text was well known to the audience. Not only were traditional texts adapted and paraphrased, but because the traditional text was well-known, there was no need specifically to attribute the saying to its original author.

Students in rhetorical schools learned how to manipulate texts such as Homer, Hesiod, Theognis, and Isocrates. They first learned simple transformations, for example, changing the introductory frames. A *chria* about the famous Cynic, Diogenes of Sinope, also appears in a school notebook, but with a different introduction:

> When mice (*mys*) crept onto the table, he [Diogenes] addressed them, "See, even Diogenes keeps parasites." (Diogenes Laertius 6.40)

> Seeing a fly (*myia*) on his table he said, "Even Diogenes keeps parasites." (*Papyrus Bouriant* I.141–68)

The notebook contains a collection of *chriae*, all introduced with the formula, "Seeing *x* he said . . ." The student had standardized all of the introductions as part of the exercise. This *chriae* reveals another small change, the shift from mice (*mys*) to fly (*myia*), but the humorous point is preserved. In both sayings

Diogenes is making fun of the social convention of wealthy persons advertising their status by having dinners with many table companions, called *parasitoi* (persons who eat at another's table). Diogenes, a penniless philosopher, boasts that he too has *parasitoi*.

Students also learned how to transform sayings by manipulating the grammar so that a saying could be framed as an affirmation, as an imperative, as a wish, or as a prohibition. A *chria* could be stated with its subject in the nominative, dative, genitive, or accusative, and thus the *chriae* could be adapted easily to any syntactical situation. But this is not all. More extensive transformation included the replacement of the vocabulary of the source saying. In some cases the transformation of the source saying is so extensive that not a single word of the source remains. The *Progymnasmata* (Preliminary Exercises) of Hermogenes (late second century CE) gives the example of the transformation of a famous maxim of Homer:

> A counseling [*boulēphoron*] man should not sleep night-long [*pannuchion*]. (*Iliad* 2.2.24, 61)
> It is not fitting for a man, proven in counsel, to sleep through the entire night. [For] a leader should always be engaged in thought, but sleep takes away counsel (Hermogenes, *Progymnasmata*)[23]

Hermogenes' paraphrase agrees with the Homeric verse in only a single Greek word, "man." The paraphrase avoids both of the unusual Homeric words (in italics) but preserves the sense of the original. But Hermogenes does something more: he also adds a rationale for the saying, explaining *why* a good counselor should not oversleep. We see here the beginnings of an argumentative elaboration.

The virtue of paraphrase was to recast a traditional saying in a form that was *apt* to the intended audience. Indeed, the duty of rhetorical paraphrase, says Quintilian, the famous first-century teacher of Latin rhetoric, "is rather to rival and vie [*aemulatio*] with the original in the expression of the same thoughts" (10.5.5). The paraphrase attempts to be as artful and appealing in its discursive context as the original was in its context. Another *Progymnasmata* by Aphthonius (fourth century CE) gives an example of a paraphrase that eliminates the florid language that was distinctive of Theognis, a sixth-century BCE gnomic poet, and reproduces the admonition in the simpler language appropriate to moral exhortation:

> One fleeing poverty, Cyrnus, must throw himself into the yawning sea and down steep crags. (Theognis 175)

> Let the one living in poverty be content to fall, for it is better to cut life short than to make the sun a witness to shame. (Aphthonius, *Progymnasmata*).[24]

Note that Theognis's saying is not only reduced in length and the colorful language omitted, but that the paraphrase introduces an *argument* by supplying a rationale for the imperative.

Rhetorical education, then, involved learning how to condense, expand, and paraphrase predecessor texts, and then to use the paraphrase to create an argument, supplying a rationale, then analogies, arguments from the contrary, examples from history or mythology, and proof texts.

With this model of education in mind, it is now possible to understand James 1:5–8. James uses what Quintilian calls a "paraphrase through expansion" (Quintilian 10.5.8). The paraphrase begins with the key verbs of Q 11:9–10, "ask" and "give," but frames these in a conditional sentence rather than an imperative. In the course of the paraphrase, the expansion occurs:

> If someone lacks wisdom let him ask [*aiteitō*] it from the God who gives to all simply and without reproach, and it will be given to him [*kai dothēsetai autō*]. (James 1:5)

James is not satisfied simply to restate Q 11:9–10 and its seemingly straightforward relationship between asking and receiving. Instead, James elaborates on both the character of God, the giver, and the petitioner. To say that God gives "simply" means that God gives without strings attached and gives without grudging. James here implicitly distinguishes God from the multitude of human patrons who, to be sure, gave gifts to their clients, but always wanted something in return and, in many cases, humiliated their poor clients.

Then James repeats the main verb, "let him ask," and now shifts to the *disposition* of the petitioner:

> But let him ask with faith, doubting nothing. (1:6a)

Then comes an analogy, drawn from the world of maritime travel:

> For the one who doubts is like the waves of the sea, blown and fanned. (1:6b)

This leads to the conclusion:

> For let not that man suppose that he shall receive something from the Lord, a double-souled man, unstable in all his ways. (1:7–8)

The simple imperative of Q, "ask and it will be given to you," is unpacked and expanded to elaborate and qualify the astonishing confidence that Q seems to express. It is true that the one who asks will receive, because God gives with unparalleled generosity. However, James also wants to underline that the petitioner must try to emulate God's simplicity or singleness. To doubt is to destroy the bond between God and the petitioner. Throughout the letter, James takes aim at what he calls the "double-souled" and unstable and those who are controlled by *epithymiai* (base) desires.

In chapter 4 James returns to this theme, now reversing the Q aphorism:

> You ask and you do not receive. (4:3a)

This illustrates another basic rhetorical technique, of arguing from the contrary. The rationale that he supplies traces the failure to receive to the passions:

Wherefore you ask badly, in order to spend on your plea-sures. (4:3b)

Again, James is concerned with the *disposition* of the petitioner. Evil or hedonistic intentions will thwart the petition.

Adultresses! Do you not know that friendship of the world is enmity to God? Whoever therefore wants to be a friend of the world becomes an enemy of God. (4:4)

The last part of James's argument is conceptually similar to Q 16:13 (on the impossibility of being a slave to God and mammon simultaneously) and is likely another paraphrase. With it, James offers a dramatic reason why prayers have failed. As long, James argues, as one is a "friend" to the world, friendship with God is impossible and hence, God's gifts cannot be received. The person who claims to be pious and is yet a friend of the world is an example of a "double-souled" person.

James, therefore, has taken two Q sayings, 11:9 and 16:13, para-phrased both, and elaborated the first by unpacking both the giver implicit in Q's saying (God), and the conditions under which the petitioner must ask. His elaboration is not so much interested in the objects for which one asks, but the state of the psyche and the dis-positions of the psyche that should be cultivated among the wise and righteous. These are concerns typical among educated Judeans influenced by Hellenistic philosophies such as Stoicism. The para-phrase of Q 16:13 also points to an upwardly mobile, probably urban, audience. Instead of using Q's metaphor of slavery—being a slave to God or to mammon—James's paraphrase recasts the dichotomy in special categories much more appealing to educated and upwardly mobile urbanites. Ritualized friendship was one of the principal mechanisms of social alliances among the elites and sub-elites. "Friendship" implied in the Hellenistic world the sharing of attributes. Those who were friends with God shared with God divine attributes such as wisdom, honor, and uprightness. Slavery by contrast carries a social stigma, and implies none of the sense of commonality that friendship implied. James, in paraphrasing and recasting Q 16:13, has elevated the social registers which the saying now addresses: not villagers and townfolk of rural Palestine, but educated or semi-educated urban dwellers in a Hellenistic city.

There is no space to survey all of the allusions to Q sayings in James and to trace the way James's paraphrases elaborate and reconfigure Q's sayings. A full examination, however, shows that in his paraphrases, James consistently focuses on the dispositions of the psyche that are either helpful or detrimental to friendship with God, and consistently reframes sayings so that they address persons of a higher social register than that presupposed by Q.[25]

Conclusion

We do not have papyrus or parchment copies of Q. It disappeared along with many other documents of the early Jesus movement. We do have echoes of Q-like collections of sayings in such documents as *1 Clement* and the *Didache*, even if there is no proof that these knew or cited Q. And we have one substantial document, the *Gospel of Thomas*, that belongs to the same genre as Q: a sayings Gospel, consisting of sayings of Jesus without a sustained narrative framework and therefore with no account of Jesus' death.

While Matthew and Luke give us the closest to verbatim copies of Q, it is the letter of James which perhaps gives us the best idea of how Q was intended to be used. It is hardly likely that those who framed and composed Q did so merely to provide a source for later writers. I have already emphasized that the culture of Jewish Palestine was an oral-scribal culture, where most people knew texts only through their oral performance. If James is an index of how Q was intended to be used, we might suggest that Q was not composed to be a *source* but rather to be a *resource*—a resource for moral exhortation and for the inculcation of an alternate *ethos*, called "the kingdom of God."

Whether those who first used Q in Jewish Palestine were as well educated and skilled in verbal transformation as James is doubtful. Nevertheless, even for its first users, Q was probably not a collection of sayings meant to be *quoted*, but as a guide and example of exhortations about the kingdom intended to be imitated and emulated.

So Q disappeared. We see it quoted and adapted by Matthew and Luke, and employed in a very different way by James. We are now in a position to be able to reconstitute this lost Sayings Gospel. It gives us a glimpse of the earliest Jesus movement in the Galilee, a *different* Gospel with a different view of Jesus' significance. It is not a dying and rising savior that we see in Q, but a sage with uncommon wisdom, wisdom that addressed the daily realities of small-town life in Jewish Galilee. Knowing about Q lets us think differently about the complexion of the early Jesus movement, differently about the development of the Synoptic Gospels, differently about the creation of documents such as the letter of James, differently about the death of Jesus and Jesus' vindication, and differently about the core and essence of the Jesus movement.

The Sayings Gospel Q in English

Sigla

{C} The International Q Project (IQP) employed a system for grading its decisions, borrowed from the United Bible Societies Greek New Testament. Each decision regarding the wording or the sequence of a Q text is grade {A}–{D}, with {A} and {B} representing a relatively high degree of confidence in reconstructing Q, and {C} and {D} much lower degrees of confidence. {C} reconstructions are signaled by the presence of double square brackets [[ ]]; {D} texts are signaled by the presence of question marks (?) enclosing the verse number. The English text is enclosed in « », to provide a general sense of what may have been in Q.

[[. . .]] Double square brackets are used to indicate a {C} degree of uncertainty in the wording of Q or, if the square brackets are placed around the pericope title, whether the pericope can be assigned to Q in the first place.

. . . Three dots indicate that there must have been some text in Q, but it cannot be reconstructed at all.

.. Two dots indicate that there may be something here in Q, but nothing can be reconstituted.

7,?10?   The question marks signal texts where there is a {D} (very low) degree of certainty concerning whether the text belongs to Q or not. While the *Critical Edition* does not venture a reconstruction of the text at all, in this translation I have given a general sense of the wording, always enclosed in « » to indicate that the wording is quite conjectural.

« »   This siglum is used when the Q text cannot be reconstructed either because the text exists in only Matthew or Luke, or because Matthew and Luke disagree completely in wording but agree in sense (see, e.g., Q 4:2).

< >   Angle brackets are used to signal an emendation in the text.

Q 3:0 Incipit

[[. . . Jesus . . .]]

Q 3:2b, 3 The Introduction of John

2b. . . John .. 3. . . all the region of the Jordan . . .

Q 3:7–9 John's Announcement of Judgment

7He said to the [[crowds coming to be]] bapti[[zed]]: Snakes' litter! Who warned you to run from the impending rage? 8So bear fruit worthy of repentance, and do not presume to tell yourselves: We have Abraham as forefather! For I tell you: God can produce children for Abraham right out of these rocks! 9And the ax already lies at the root of the trees. So every tree not bearing healthy fruit is to be chopped down and thrown on the fire.

Q 3:16b–17 John and the One to Come

16bI baptize you [[in]] water, but the one to come after me is more powerful than I, whose sandals I am not fit to [[take off]]. He will baptize you in [[holy]] Spirit and fire. 17His pitchfork «is» in his hand, and he will clear his threshing floor and gather the wheat into his granary, but the chaff he will burn on a fire that can never be put out.

{[[Q 3:21–22 The Baptism of Jesus]]} [1]

[21]{[[. . . Jesus . . . baptized, heaven opened .. , [22]and .. the Spirit . . . upon him . . . Son. . . .]]}

Q 4:1–4, 9–12, 5–8, 13 The Temptations of Jesus

[1]And Jesus was led [[into]] the wilderness by the Spirit [2][[to be]] tempted by the devil. And «he ate nothing» for forty days, .. he became hungry. [3]And the devil told him: If you are God's Son, order that these stones become loaves. [4]And Jesus answered [[him]]: It is written: A person is not to live only from bread.

[9][[The devil]] took him along to Jerusalem and put him on the tip of the temple and told him: If you are God's Son, throw yourself down. [10]For it is written: He will command his angels about you, [11]and on their hands they will bear you, so that you do not strike your foot against a stone. [12]And Jesus [[in reply]] told him: It is written: Do not put to the test the Lord your God.

[5]And the devil took him along to a [[very high]] mountain and showed him all the kingdoms of the world and their splendor, [6]and told him: All these I will give you, [7]if you bow down before me. [8]And [[in reply]] Jesus told him: It is written: Bow down to the Lord your God, and serve only him.

[13]And the devil left him.

Q 4:16 Nazara

[16]. . . Nazara . . .

Q 6:20–21 The Beatitudes for the Poor, Hungry, and Mourning

[20]. . . And [[rais]]ing his [[eyes to]] his disciples he said: Blessed are [[«you»]] poor, for God's reign is for [[you]]. [21]Blessed are

[[«you»]] who hunger, for [[you]] will eat [[your]] fill. Blessed are [[«you»]] who [[mourn]], for [[‹you› will be consoled]].

Q 6:22–23 The Beatitude for the Persecuted

²²Blessed are you when they insult and [[persecute]] you, and [[say every kind of]] evil [[against]] you because of the son of man. ²³Be glad and [[exult]], for vast is your recompense in heaven. For this is how they [[persecuted]] the prophets who «were» before you.

Q 6:?24–26? The Woes

?24?«But woe to you that are rich, for you have received your consolation.» ?25?«Woe to you that are full now, for you shall hunger. Woe to you that laugh now, for you shall mourn and weep.» ?26?«Woe to you, when all men speak well of you, for so their fathers did to the false prophets.»²

Q 6:27–28, 35c–d Love Your Enemies

²⁷Love your enemies ²⁸[[and]] pray for those [[persecuting]] you, ³⁵ᶜ⁻ᵈso that you may become sons of your Father, for he raises his sun on bad and [[good and rains on the just and unjust]].

Q 6:29–30 Renouncing One's Own Rights

²⁹[[The one who slaps]] you on the cheek, offer [[him]] the other as well; and [[to the person wanting to take you to court and get]] your shirt, [[turn over to him]] the coat as well. Q/Matt 5:41[[«And the one who conscripts you for one mile, go with him a second.»]] ³⁰To the one who asks of you, give; and [[from the one who borrows, do not [[ask]] back [[«what is»]] yours.

Q 6:31 The Golden Rule

³¹And the way you want people to treat you, that is how you treat them.

Q 6:32, 34 Impartial Love

³².. If you love those loving you, what reward do you have? Do not even tax collectors do the same? ³⁴And if you [[lend «to those» from whom you hope to receive, what ‹reward do› you ‹have›]]? Do not even [[the Gentiles]] do the same?

Q 6:36 Being Full of Pity Like Your Father

³⁶Be merciful, just as your Father .. is merciful.

Q 6:37–38 Not Judging

³⁷.. Do not pass judgment, «so» you are not judged. [[For with what judgment you pass judgment, you will be judged.]] ³⁸[[And]] with the measure you use to measure out, it will be measured back to you.

Q 6:39 The Blind Leading the Blind

³⁹Can a blind person show the way to a blind person? Will not both fall into a pit?

Q 6:40 The Disciple and the Teacher

⁴⁰A disciple is not superior to «one's» teacher. [[It is enough for the disciple that he become]] like his teacher.

Q 6:41–42 The Speck and the Beam

⁴¹And why do you see the speck in your brother's eye, but the beam in your own eye you overlook? ⁴²How «can you say» to your brother: Let me throw out the speck [[from]] your eye, and just look at the beam in your own eye? Hypocrite, first throw out from your own eye the beam, and then you will see clearly to throw out the speck «in» your brother's eye.

Q 6:43–45 The Tree Is Known by Its Fruit

⁴³.. No healthy tree bears rotten fruit, nor [[on the other hand]] does a decayed tree bear healthy fruit. ⁴⁴For from the fruit the tree is known. Are figs picked from thorns, or grape[[s]] from thistles? ⁴⁵The good person from «one's» good treasure casts up good things, and the evil [[person]] from the evil [[treasure]] casts up evil things. For from exuberance of heart [[one's]] mouth speaks.

Q 6:46 Not Just Saying Master, Master

⁴⁶.. Why do you call me: Master, Master, and do not do what I say?

Q 6:47–49 Houses Built on Rock or Sand

⁴⁷Everyone hearing my words and acting on them .. ⁴⁸is like a person who built [[one's]] house on bedrock; and the rain poured down and the flash-floods came, [[and the winds blew]] and pounded that house, and it did not collapse, for it was founded on bedrock. ⁴⁹And [[everyone]] who hears [[my words]] and does not act on [[them]] is like a person who built [[one's]] house on the sand; and the rain poured down and the flash-floods came, [[and the winds blew]] and battered that house, and promptly it collapsed, and its [[fall]] was devastating.

Q 7:1, 3, 6b–9, 10 The Centurion's Faith in Jesus' Word

¹[[And it came to pass when]] he .. ended these sayings, he entered Capernaum. ³There came to him a centurion exhorting him [[and saying: My]] boy [[‹is› doing badly. And he said to him: Am I]], by coming, to heal him? ⁶ᵇ⁻ᶜAnd in reply the centurion said: Master, I am not worthy for you to come under my roof; ⁷but say a word, and [[let]] my boy [[be]] healed. ⁸For I too am a person under authority, with soldiers under me, and I say to one: Go, and he goes, and to another: Come, and he comes, and to my slave: Do this, and he does «it». ⁹But Jesus, on hearing, was amazed, and said

to those who followed: I tell you, not even in Israel have I found such faith. [10]«‹And the serving boy was healed.›»[3]

Q 7:18–23 *John's Inquiry about the One to Come*

[18]And John, on hearing .. [[about all these things]], [19]sending through his disciples, [[said]] to him: Are you the one to come, or are we to expect someone else? [22]And in reply he said to them: Go report to John what you hear and see: blind regain their sight and lame walk around, skin-diseased are cleansed and deaf hear, dead are raised, and the poor are given good news. [23]And blessed is whoever is not offended by me.

Q 7:24–28 *John—More than a Prophet*

[24]And when they had left, he began to talk to the crowds about John: What did you go out into the wilderness to look at? A reed shaken by the wind? [25]If not, what *did* you go out to see? A person arrayed in finery? Look, those wearing finery are in kings' houses. [26]But «then» what did you go out to see? A prophet? Yes, I tell you, even more than a prophet! [27]This is the one about whom it has been written: Look, I am sending my messenger ahead of you, who will prepare your path in front of you. [28]I tell you: There has not arisen among women's offspring «anyone» who surpasses John. Yet the least significant in God's kingdom is more than he.

[[Q 7:29–30 *For and against John*]]

[29][[«For John came to you» .. , . . . the tax collectors and . . . «responded positively»,]] [30][[but «the religious authorities rejected» him.]]

Q 7:31–35 *This Generation and the Children of Wisdom*

[31].. To what am I to compare this generation and what ‹is it› like? [32]It is like children seated in [[the]] market-place[[s]], who,

addressing [[the others]], say: We fluted for you, but you would not dance; we wailed, but you would not cry. [33]For John came, neither eating nor drinking, and you say: He has a demon! [34]The son of man came, eating and drinking, and you say: Look! A person «who is» a glutton and drunkard, a friend of tax collectors and sinners! [35]But Wisdom was vindicated by her children.

Q 9:57–60, ?61–62? *Confronting Potential Followers*

[57]And someone said to him: I will follow you wherever you go. [58]And Jesus said to him: Foxes have holes, and birds of the sky have nests; but the son of man does not have anywhere he can lay his head. [59]But another said to him: Master, permit me first to go and bury my father. [60]But he said to him: Follow me, and leave the dead to bury their own dead. [61]«Another said, I will follow you, Lord; but let me first say farewell to those at my home.» [62]«Jesus said to him, No one who puts a hand to the plow and looks back is fit for the kingdom of God.»[4]

Q 10:2 *Workers for the Harvest*

[2]He said to his disciples: The harvest is plentiful, but the day laborers are few. So ask the Lord of the harvest to dispatch day laborers into his harvest.

Q 10:3 *Sheep among Wolves*

[3]Be on your way! Look, I send you like sheep in the midst of wolves.

Q 10:4 *No Provisions*

[4]Carry no [[purse]], not knapsack, nor sandals, nor stick, and greet no one on the road.

Q 10:5–9 *What to Do in Houses and Towns*

[5]Into whatever house you enter, [[first]] say: Peace [[to this house]]! [6]And if a son of peace be there, let your peace come upon him; but

if not, [[let]] your peace [[return upon]] you. [7][[And at that house]] remain, «eating and drinking whatever they provide», for the day laborer is worthy of his wages. [[Do not move around from house to house.]] [8]And whatever town you enter and they take you in, [[«eat what is set before you»]]. [9]And cure the sick there, and say [[to them]]: The kingdom of God has reached unto you.

Q 10:10–12 Response to a Town's Rejection

[10]But into whatever town you enter and they do not take you in, on going out [[from that town]], [11]shake off the dust from your feet. [12]I tell you: For Sodom it shall be more bearable on that day than for that town.

Q 10:13–15, Q/Matt 11:?23b–24? Woes against Galilean Towns

[13] Woe to you, Chorazin! Woe to you, Bethsaida! For if the wonders performed in you had taken place in Tyre and Sidon, they would have repented long ago, in sackcloth and ashes. [14]Yet for Tyre and Sidon it shall be more bearable at the judgment than for you. [15]And you, Capernaum, up to heaven will you be exalted? Into Hades shall you come down! [Q/Matt 11:?23b?]«For if the mighty works done in you had been done in Sodom, it would have remained until this day.» [Q/Matt 11:?24?]«But I tell you that it shall be more tolerable on the day of judgment for the land of Sodom than for you.»[5]

Q 10:16 Whoever Takes You In Takes Me In

[16]Whoever receives you receives me, [[and]] whoever receives me receives the one who sent me.

Q 10:21 Thanksgiving That God Reveals Only to Children

[21]At «that time» he said: I thank you, Father, Lord of heaven and earth, for you hid these things from sages and the learned, and disclosed them to children. Yes, Father, for that is what it has pleased you to do.

Q 10:22 Knowing the Father through the Son

²²Everything has been entrusted to me by my Father, and no one knows the Son except the Father, nor [[does anyone know]] the Father except the Son, and to whomever the Son chooses to reveal him.

Q 10:23–24 The Beatitude for the Eyes That See

²³Blessed are the eyes that see what you see ... . ²⁴For I tell you: Many prophets and kings wanted to see what you see, but never saw it, and to hear what you hear, but never heard it.

Q 11:2b–4 The Lord's Prayer

²ᵇ[[When]] you pray, [[say]]: Father—may your name be kept holy!—let your reign come: ³Give us our daily bread today; ⁴and cancel our debts for us, as we too have cancelled for those in debt to us; and do not put us to the test!

Q 11:9–13 The Certainty of the Answer to Prayer

⁹I tell you, ask and it will be given to you, search and you will find, knock and it will be opened to you. ¹⁰For everyone who asks receives, and the one who searches finds, and to the one who knocks will it be opened. ¹¹.. What person of you, whose son asks for bread, will give him a stone? ¹²Or again when he asks for a fish, will give him a snake? ¹³So if you, though evil, know how to give good gifts to your children, how much more will the Father from heaven give good things to those who ask him!

Q 11:14–15, 17–20 Refuting the Beelzebul Accusation

¹⁴And he cast out a demon «which made a person» mute. And once the demon was cast out, the mute person spoke. And the crowds were amazed. ¹⁵But some said: By Beelzebul, the ruler of demons, he casts out demons! ¹⁷But, knowing their thoughts, he said to them: Every kingdom divided against itself is left barren,

and every household divided against itself will not stand. ¹⁸And if Satan is divided against himself, how will his kingdom stand? ¹⁹And if I by Beelzebul cast out demons, your sons, by whom do they cast «them» out? This is why they will be your judges. ²⁰But if it is by the finger of God that I cast out demons, then there has come upon you God's reign.

[[Q 11:21–22 Looting a Strong Person]]

²¹[[«A strong person's house cannot be looted,»]] ²²[[«but if someone still stronger overpowers him, he does get looted.»]]

Q 11:23 The One Not with Me

²³The one not with me is against me, and the one not gathering with me scatters.

Q 11:24–26 The Return of the Unclean Spirit

²⁴When the defiling spirit has left the person, it wanders through waterless regions looking for a resting-place, and finds none. [[Then]] it says, I will return to my house from which I came. ²⁵And on arrival it finds «it» swept and tidied up. ²⁶Then it goes and brings with it seven other spirits more evil than itself, and, moving in, they settle there. And the last «circumstances» of that person become worse than the first.

Q 11:?27–28? ?Hearing and Keeping God's Word?

^{?27?}«While he was saying this, a woman in the crowd raised her voice and said to him: Blessed is the womb that bore you and the breasts that nursed you!» ^{?28?}«But he said: Blessed rather are those who hear the word of God and obey it!»⁶

Q 11:16, 29–30 The Sign of Jonah for This Generation

¹⁶[[But]] some .. were demanding from him a sign. ²⁹But .. [[he said]] .. : This generation is an evil .. generation; it demands a sign,

and a sign will not be given to it—except the sign of Jonah! ³⁰For as Jonah became to the Ninevites a sign, so [[also]] will the son of man be to this generation.

Q 11:31–32 Something More Than Solomon and Jonah

³¹The queen of the South will be raised at the judgment with this generation and condemn it, for she came from the ends of the earth to listen to the wisdom of Solomon, and look, something more than Solomon is here! ³²Ninevite men will arise at the judgment with this generation and condemn it. For they repented at the preaching of Jonah, and look, something more than Jonah is here!

Q 11:33 The Light on the Lampstand

³³No one light‹s› a lamp and puts it [[in a hidden place]], but on the lampstand, [[and it gives light for everyone in the house]].

Q 11:34–35 The Jaundiced Eye Darkens the Body's Light

³⁴The lamp of the body is the eye. If your eye is generous, your whole body [[is]] radiant; but if your eye is jaundiced, your whole body «is» dark. ³⁵So if the light within you is dark, how great «must» the darkness «be»!

Q 11:?39a?, 42, 39b, 41, 43–44 Woes against the Pharisees

?39a?.. ⁴²Woe for you, Pharisees, for you tithe mint and dill and cumin, and [[give up]] justice and mercy and faithfulness. But these one has to do, without giving up those. ³⁹ᵇWoe to you, Pharisees, for you purify the outside of the cup and dish, but inside [[they are]] full of plunder and dissipation. ⁴¹[[Purify]] .. the inside of the cup, . . . its outside . . . pure. ⁴³Woe to you, Pharisees, for ‹you› love [[the place of honor at banquets and]] the front seat in the synagogues and accolades in the markets. ⁴⁴Woe to you,

[[Pharisees,]] for you are like indistinct tombs, and people walking on top are unaware.

Q 11:46b, 52, 47–48 Woes against the Exegetes of the Law

⁴⁶ᵇ[[And]] woe to you, [[exegetes of the Law,]] for ‹you› [[bind]] . . . burdens, [[and load on the backs of people, but]] ‹you your›selves do not [[want «to lift»]] your finger [[to move]] them. ⁵²Woe to you, [[exegetes of the Law,]] for you shut the [[kingdom of ‹God› from people]]; you did not go in, [[nor]] let in those «trying to» get in. ⁴⁷Woe to you, for you built the tombs of the prophets, but your «fore»fathers killed them. ⁴⁸«Thus» [[you]] witness [[against yourselves that]] you are [[sons]] of your «fore»fathers. ..

Q 11:49–51 Wisdom's Judgment on This Generation

⁴⁹Therefore also .. Wisdom said: I will send them prophets and sages, and «some» of them they will kill and persecute, ⁵⁰so that «a settling of accounts for» the blood of all the prophets poured out from the founding of the world may be required of this generation, ⁵¹from «the» blood of Abel to «the» blood of Zechariah, murdered between the sacrificial altar and the House. Yes, I tell you, «an accounting» will be required of this generation!

Q 12:2–3 Proclaiming What Was Whispered

²Nothing is covered up that will not be exposed, and hidden that will not be known. ³What I say to you in the dark, speak in the light; and what you hear «whispered» in the ear, proclaim on the housetops.

Q 12:4–5 Not Fearing the Body's Death

⁴And do not be afraid of those who kill the body, but cannot kill the soul. ⁵But fear .. the one who is able to destroy both the soul and body in Gehenna.

Q 12:6–7 More Precious Than Many Sparrows

[6]Are not [[five]] sparrows sold for [[two]] *assaria*? And yet not one of them will fall to earth without [[your Father's]] «consent». [7]But even the hairs of your head all are numbered. Do not be afraid, you are worth more than many sparrows.

Q 12:8–9 Confessing or Denying

[8]Anyone who [[may]] speak out for me in public, [[the son of man]] will also speak out for him before the angels .. . [9]But whoever may deny me in public [[will be]] den[[ied]] before the angels .. .

Q 12:10 Speaking against the Holy Spirit

[10]And whoever says a word against the son of man, it will be forgiven him; but whoever [[speaks]] against the holy Spirit, it will not be forgiven him.

Q 12:11–12 Hearings before Synagogues

[11]When they bring you before synagogues, do not be anxious about how or what you are to say; [12]for [[the holy Spirit will teach]] you in that .. hour what you are to say.

?Q 12:13–14? Who Made me a Divider?[7]

[?13?]«One of the crowd said to him: Teacher, tell my brother to divide with me the inheritance. [?14?]But he said to him: Fellow, who made me a judge or divider over you?»

?Q 12:16–21? A Rich Fool

[?16?]«And he said to them: The land of a rich man brought forth plentifully [?17?]and he thought to himself: What shall I do, for I have nowhere to store my crops? [?18?]And he said, I will do this: I will pull down my barns, and build larger ones; and there I will store all my grain and my goods. [?19?]And I will say to my soul, Soul, you have ample goods laid up for many years; take your ease, eat, drink, be merry. ²²⁰°But God said to him, Fool! This night your soul is required of you; and the things you have prepared, whose will they be? ²²¹°'Thus is the one who lays up treasure for himself and is not rich toward God.»

Q 12:22b–31 *Free from Anxiety Like Ravens and Lilies*

²²ᵇTherefore I tell you, do not be anxious about your life, what you are to eat, nor about your body, with what you are to clothe yourself. ²³Is not life more than food, and the body than clothing? ²⁴Consider the ravens: They neither sow nor reap nor gather into barns, and yet God feeds them. Are you not better than the birds? ²⁵And who of you by being anxious is able to add to one's stature a .. cubit? ²⁶And why are you anxious about clothing? ²⁷[[Observe]] the lilies, how they grow: They do not work nor do they spin. Yet I tell you: Not even Solomon in all his glory was arrayed like one of these. ²⁸But if in the field the grass, there today and tomorrow thrown into the oven, God clothes thus, will he not much more clothe you, persons of petty faith! ²⁹[[So]] do not be anxious, saying: What are we to eat? [[Or:]] What are we to drink? [[Or:]] What are we to wear? ³⁰For all these the Gentiles seek; [[for]] your Father knows that you need them [[all]]. ³¹But seek his kingdom, and [[all]] these shall be granted to you.

Q 12:33–34 *Storing Up Treasures in Heaven*[8]

³³«Do not treasure for yourselves treasures on earth, where moth and gnawing deface and where robbers dig through and rob,» but treasure for yourselves treasure«s» in heaven, where neither moth nor gnawing defaces and where robbers do not dig through nor rob. ³⁴For where your treasure is, there will also be your heart.

Q 12:39–40 *The Son of Humanity Comes as a Robber*

³⁹But know [[this]]: If the householder had known in which watch the robber was coming, he would not have let his house be dug

into. [40]You also must be ready, for the Son of man is coming at an hour you do not expect.

Q 12:42–46 The Faithful or Unfaithful Slave

[42]Who then is the faithful [[and]] wise slave whom the master put over his household to give [[them]] food on time? [43]Blessed is that slave whose master, on coming, will find so doing. [44][[Amen]], I tell you, he will appoint him over all his possessions. [45]But if that slave says in his heart: My master is delayed, and begins to beat [[his fellow slaves]], and eats and drinks [[with the]] drunk[[ards]], [46]the master of that slave will come on a day he does not expect and at an hour he does not know, and will cut him to pieces and give him an inheritance with the faithless.

Q 12:[[49]], 51, 53 Children against Parents

[49][[«Fire have I come to hurl on the earth, and how I wish it had already blazed up!»]] [51][[Do you]] think that I have come to hurl peace on earth? I did not come to hurl peace, but a sword! [53]For I have come to divide son against father, [[and]] daughter against her mother, [[and]] daughter-in-law against her mother-in-law.

[[Q 12:54–56 Judging the Time]]

[54][[«But he said to them:» When evening has come, you say: Good weather! For the sky is flame red.]] [55][[And at dawn: Today «it's» wintry! For the lowering sky is flame red.]] [56][[The face of the sky you know to interpret, but the time you are not able to?]]

Q 12:58–59 Settling out of Court

[58][[While]] you «go along» with your opponent on the way, make an effort to get loose from him, lest [[the opponent]] hand you over to the judge, and the judge to the assistant, and [[the «assis-

tant>]] throw [[you]] into prison. ⁵⁹I say to you: You will not get out of there until you pay the last *[[quadrans]]*.

Q 13:18–19 The Parable of the Mustard Seed

¹⁸What is the kingdom of God like, and with what am I to compare it? ¹⁹It is like a seed of mustard, which a person took and threw into his [[garden]]. And it grew and developed into a tree, and the birds of the sky nested in its branches.

Q 13:20–21 The Parable of the Yeast

²⁰[[And again]]: With what am I to compare the kingdom of God? ²¹It is like yeast, which a woman took «and» hid in three measures of flour until it was fully fermented.

Q 13:24–27 I Do Not Know You

²⁴Enter through the narrow door, for many will seek to enter and few [[are those who ‹enter through› it]]. ²⁵When the [[householder has arisen]] and locked the door, [[and you begin to stand outside and knock on the door,]] saying: Master, open for us, and he will answer you: I do not know you. ²⁶Then you will begin saying: We ate in your presence and drank, and «it was» in our streets you taught. ²⁷And he will say to you: I do not know you! Get away from me, [[you who]] do lawlessness!

Q 13:29, 28 Replaced by People from East and West

²⁹[[And many]] shall come from Sunrise and Sunset and recline ²⁸with Abraham and Isaac and Jacob in the kingdom of God, but [[you will be]] thrown out [[into the]] out[[er darkness]], where there will be wailing and grinding of teeth.

[[Q 13:30 The Reversal of the Last and the First]]

³⁰[[.. The last will be first and the first last.]]

Q 13:34–35 Judgment over Jerusalem

³⁴O Jerusalem, Jerusalem, who kills the prophets and stones those sent to her! How often I wanted to gather your children together, as a hen gathers her nestlings under her wings, and you were not willing! ³⁵Look, your house is forsaken! .. I tell you, you will not see me until [[«the time» comes when]] you say: Blessed is the one who comes in the name of the Lord!

[[Q 14:11 The Exalted Humbled and the Humble Exalted]]

¹¹[[Everyone exalting oneself will be humbled, and the one humbling oneself will be exalted.]]

Q 14:16–18, ?19–20?, 21, 23 The Parable of the Invited Dinner Guests

¹⁶A certain person prepared a [[large]] dinner, [[and invited many]]. ¹⁷And he sent his slave [[at the time of the dinner]] to say to the invited: Come, for it is now ready. ¹⁸«One declined because of his» farm. ?¹⁹?«Another declined because of his business.» ?²⁰?«A third declined . . .». ²¹«And the slave, ‹on coming, said› these things to his master.» Then the householder, enraged, said to his slave: ²³Go out on the roads, and whomever you find, invite, so that my house may be filled.

Q 14:26 Hating One's Family

²⁶[[‹The one who›]] does not hate father and mother ‹can›not ‹be› my ‹disciple›; and [[‹the one who›]] ‹does not hate› son and daughter cannot be my disciple.

Q 14:27 Taking One's Cross

²⁷.. The one who does not take one's cross and follow after me cannot be my disciple.

Q 17:33 Losing One's Life

³³[[The one who]] finds one's life will lose it, and [[the one who]] loses one's life [[for my sake]] will find it.

Q 14:34–35 Insipid Salt

³⁴Salt [[is good]]; but if salt becomes insipid, with what will it be [[seasoned]]? ³⁵Neither for the earth nor for the dunghill is it [[fit]] —it gets thrown out.

Q 16:13 God or Mammon

¹³No one can be a slave to two owners; for a person will either hate the one and love the other, or be devoted to the one and despise the other. You cannot be a slave to God and Mammon.

Q 16:16 Since John the Kingdom of God

¹⁶.. The law and the prophets «were» until John. From then «on» the kingdom of God is violated and the violent plunder it.

Q 16:17 No Serif of the Law to Fall

¹⁷[[But it is easier for]] heaven and earth [[to]] pass away [[than for one iota or]] one serif of the law [[to fall]].

Q 16:18 Divorce Leading to Adultery

¹⁸Everyone who divorces his wife [[and marries another]] commits adultery, and the one who marries a divorcée commits adultery.

Q 17:1–2 Against Enticing Little Ones

¹It is necessary for offenses to come, but woe «to the one» through whom they come! ²It is better for him [[if]] a millstone is

put around his neck and he is thrown into the sea, than that he should offend one of these little ones.

Q 15:4–5a, 7 The Lost Sheep

⁴Which person «is there» among you «who» has a hundred sheep, [[on losing]] one of them, [[will]] not leave the ninety-nine [[in the mountains]] and go [[hunt for]] the [[lost one]]? ⁵ᵃAnd if it should happen that he finds it, ⁷I say to you that he rejoices over it more than over the ninety-nine that did not go astray.

[[Q 15:8–10 The Lost Coin]]

⁸[[«Or what woman who has ten coins, if she were to lose one coin, would not light a lamp and sweep the house and hunt until she finds?» ⁹«And on finding she calls the friends and neighbors, saying: Rejoice with me, for I found the coin which I lost.» ¹⁰«Just so, I tell you, there is joy before the angels over one repenting sinner.»]]

Q 17:3–4 Forgiving a Sinning Brother Repeatedly

³If your brother sins [[against you]], rebuke him; and if [[he repents]], forgive him. ⁴And if seven times a day he sins against you, also seven times shall you forgive him.

Q 17:6 Faith Like a Mustard Seed

⁶If you have faith like a mustard seed, you might say to this mulberry tree: Be uprooted and planted in the sea! And it would obey you.

[[Q 17:20–21 The Kingdom of God within You]]

²⁰[[«But on being asked when the kingdom of God is coming, he answered them and said: The kingdom of God is not coming visibly.»]] ²¹[[«Nor will one say:» Look, here! or: «There! For, look, the kingdom of God is among you!»]]

Q 17:23–24 The Son of Man Like Lightning

²³If they say to you: Look, he is in the wilderness, do not go out; look, he is indoors, do not follow. ²⁴For as the lightning streaks out from Sunrise and flashes as far as Sunset, so will be the Son of man [[on his day]].

Q 17:37 *Vultures around a Corpse*

³⁷Wherever the corpse, there the vultures will gather.

Q 17:26–27, ?28–29?, 30 As in the Days of Noah

²⁶.. [[As it took place in]] the days of Noah, so will it be [[in the day]] of the Son of man. ²⁷[[For as in those days]] they were eating and drinking, marrying and giving in marriage, until the day Noah entered the ark and the flood came and took them all, ?²⁸«Likewise, as it was in the days of Lot: they were eating and drinking, buying and selling, planting and building» ²⁹?«but on the day that Lot left Sodom, it rained fire and sulfur from heaven and destroyed all of them»,⁹ ³⁰so will it also be on the day the Son of man is revealed.

Q 17:34–35 One Taken, One Left

³⁴I tell you, there will be two [[in the field]]; one is taken and one is left. ³⁵Two women will be grinding at the mill; one is taken and one is left.

Q 19:12–13, 15–24, 26 The Parable of the Entrusted Money

¹².. A certain person, on taking a trip, ¹³called ten of his slaves and gave them ten minas and said to them: Do business until I come. ¹⁵.. [[After a long time]] the master of those slaves comes and settles accounts with them. ¹⁶And the first [[came]] saying: Master, your mina has produced ten more minas. ¹⁷And he said to him: Well done, good slave, you have been faithful over a pittance, I

will set you over much. ¹⁸And the [[second]] came saying: Master, your mina has earned five minas. ¹⁹He said [[to him: Well done, good slave, you have been faithful over a pittance,]] I will set you over much. ²⁰And the other came saying: Master, ²¹[[I knew]] you, that you are a hard person, reaping where you did not sow and gathering from where you did not winnow; and, scared, I [[went and]] hid [[your mina]] in [[the ground]]. Here, you have what belongs to you. ²²He said to him: Wicked slave! You knew that I reap where I have not sown, and gather from where I have not winnowed? ²³[[Then you had to invest]] my money [[with the]] moneychangers]]! And at my coming I would have received what belongs to me plus interest. ²⁴So take from him the mina and give «to» the one who has the ten minas. ²⁶[[For]] to everyone who has will be given; but from the one who does not have, even what he has will be taken from him.

Q 22:28, 30 *You Will Judge the Twelve Tribes of Israel*

²⁸.. You who have followed me ³⁰will sit .. on thrones judging the twelve tribes of Israel.

Glossary

2DH   *See* Two Document hypothesis.

2GH   *See* Two Gospel hypothesis.

4SH   *See* Four Source hypothesis.

assarion, assaria.   A small Roman coin worth from one-tenth to one-sixteenth of a denarius. Typically said to be the value of one hour's work.

catchword.   Catchword composition refers to the assembling of sayings on the basis of a common word or phrase. For example, Proverbs 12:15 "The way of a *fool* is right in his own eyes, but a wise man listens to advice." 12:16 "The vexation of a *fool* is known at once, but the prudent man ignores an insult."

catena.   From the Latin for "chain," a catena is a collection or assembly of similar items. *Didache* 1.3b–5 is a catena of short sayings of Jesus, all in the imperative.

Chester Beatty I.   One of eleven biblical and parabiblical manuscripts held by the Chester Beatty Library in Dublin. Chester Beatty I or $\mathfrak{P}^{45}$ is a mid-third century CE containing our earliest copy of the Gospel of Mark.

chria, chriae.   According to Aelius Theon of Alexandria, a chria is a "brief statement or action fittingly attributed to a definite person or something analogous to a person." This is the ancient rhetorical designation for what have later been termed "apophthegms" or "pronouncement stories" and include declaratory (NN said, . . .), responsive (being asked about *x*, NN replied, . . .) and circumstantial forms (seeing *x*, NN said, . . .).

deutero-Markus.   A hypothesis that posits two versions of Mark, a version of Mark very similar to canonical Mark, and a secondary development of Mark used by Matthew and Luke. The deutero-Markus hypothesis serves as one way to account for certain problematic features of the synoptic tradition, in

145

particular the "minor agreements" of Matthew and Luke against Mark.

Didache.   A treatise in sixteen chapters, representing the oldest extant church manual. The treatise contains a moral exhortation structured around the trope of two contrasting roads, instructions on baptism, the Eucharist, the reception of traveling "apostles" and "prophets" and other matters of church order, and a concluding apocalypse. The *Didache* was likely composed in the late first century CE and edited in the mid-second century.

Double tradition.   Synoptic pericopae found in Matthew and Luke, but not in Mark (e.g., Matt 3:7–10 || Luke 3:7–9), or where Mark's form is significantly different from those of Matthew and Luke (e.g., Matt 4:1–11 || Luke 4:1–13; cf. Mark 1:12–13).

Farrer-Goulder hypothesis.   *See* Mark without Q hypothesis.

Four Source hypothesis (4SH).   Associated with B. H. Streeter, this hypothesis is a form of the Two Document hypothesis. In addition to asserting the priority of Mark and Q, the 4SH accounts for special Matthean material by means of a discrete document (M) and special Lukan material by a fourth source, L. This theory is now generally abandoned, since it is impossible to show that either M or L were documents.

GH, Griesbach hypothesis.   *See* Two Gospel hypothesis.

IQP   The International Q Project, with a membership of thirty Q specialists from the United States, Canada, Germany, the United Kingdom, Finland, and South Africa. Established by the Society of Biblical Literature to edit a critical edition of Q and a comprehensive database on the reconstruction of Q.

kerygma.   Meaning "proclamation," this usually refers to the Christian proclamation of the saving effects of the death and resurrection of Jesus. The term appears in Q (11:32) simply meaning "preaching."

Kinneret.   The Sea of Galilee, not a sea at all, but a large freshwater lake. The name Kinneret comes from the Hebrew word *kinnor* ("harp") and describes the shape of the lake.

makarism.   From Greek *makarios*, "blessing," "beatitude."

Mark without Q hypothesis (MwQH).   Associated with Austin Farrer, Michael Goulder, and Mark Goodacre, this hypothesis holds that Mark was the first Gospel, Matthew expanded Mark, and Luke used both Mark and Matthew.

mimesis.   From Greek meaning "imitation." In literature, the imitation (rather than simple copying) of one work by another.

Minimal Q.   Those portions of the double tradition where there is verbatim agreement between Matthew and Luke and hence a very high degree of confidence as to the original wording of Q.

minor agreements.   Aspects of Matthew and Luke where they agree *against Mark*. These include both "negative agreements," where Matthew and Luke in common omit portions of Mark, and "positive agreements," where Matthew and Luke have grammatical formulations or vocabulary not present in Mark.

MwQH.   *See* Mark without Q hypothesis.

Oxyrhynchus papyri.   A large cache of papyri discovered in a garbage dump by B. P. Grenfell and A. S. Hunt in 1896–7 and 1903. Among the several hundred thousand papyri fragments—only 5,000 have been published to date—are texts of classical Greek authors, biblical texts, hitherto unknown Christian apocrypha, and thousands of private documents, letters, tax receipts, leases, accounts, and so forth.

parataxis.   A style of composition that favors show sentences joined by "and." Better Greek style favors longer "periodic" sentences, with a greater use made of subordination of clauses.

patrilocal.   From social anthropology, a term denoting a form of family structure in which a married couple will live with or in proximity to the husband's family, thus bringing the wife into close contact with her mother-in-law.

periocope, pericopae.   From Greek "to cut around." A group of sentences that forms a coherent unit. Used to designate a short passage suitable for liturgical reading.

quadrans.   A small Roman coin, worth one-quarter of an *assarion*.

seriatim.   From Latin "in a series."

siglum, sigla.   A sign, mark, or abbreviation used in the editing of critical editions of ancient texts to indicate to the reader the presence of alternate readings, gaps in the text (*lacunae*), additions, erasures, uncertain readings, and so forth.

Special material, *Sondergut*.   Sayings or stories that are peculiar to one evangelist (e.g., the parable of the Prodigal Son [Luke 10:30–37]).

Triple tradition.   Synoptic pericopae found in all three Synoptics (e.g., the baptism of Jesus, Mark 1:9–11 || Matt 3:13–17 || Luke 3:21–22).

Two Document hypothesis (2DH).   First proposed in 1838 and held
by most Synoptic scholars today, the hypothesis affirms the priority of Mark and the independent use of Mark by Matthew and
Luke. This requires as a corollary the positing of a second
source beside Mark in order to account for the "double tradition." This source is now called "Q" or the "Sayings Gospel Q."
Sometimes called the Two Source hypothesis or Two Source
theory.

Two Gospel hypothesis (GH; Owen-Griesbach hypothesis; 2GH).
Associated with Henry Owen and J. J. Griesbach, the hypoth-
esis holds that Matthew is the first Gospel to be written, that
Luke used Matthew, and that Mark conflated and abbreviated
Matthew and Luke. The modern revival of the GH prefers the
name Two Gospel hypothesis (2GH).

Ur-Markus.   A theory which holds that the canonical Gospel of
Mark was composed from an earlier version of Mark (*Ur-
Markus* or "original Mark"), often thought to be longer than
canonical Mark and containing such materials as Luke 3:7–9,
16–17; 4:1–13; and 6:20b–49. The hypothesis was decisively
rejected by Paul Wernle in 1899 but has more recently reap-
peared, either in connection with resolving the problem of the
"minor agreements" or as part of the effort to understand the
relationship of the Longer (Secret) Gospel of Mark to canonical Mark.

Further Readings

Primary Texts

Aland, Kurt. *Synopsis of the Four Gospels: Completely Revised on the Basis of the Greek Text of the Nestle-Aland 26th Edition*. New York: United Bible Societies, 1982.

Kloppenborg, John S. *Q Parallels: Synopsis, Critical Notes, & Concordance*. Foundations and Facets: New Testament. Sonoma, CA: Polebridge Press, 1988.

Robinson, James M., Paul Hoffmann, and John S. Kloppenborg, eds. *The Critical Edition of Q: A Synopsis, Including the Gospels of Matthew and Luke, Mark and Thomas, with English, German and French Translations of Q and Thomas*. Hermeneia Supplements. Leuven: Peeters; Minneapolis: Fortress Press, 2000.

Robinson, James M., Paul Hoffmann, and John S. Kloppenborg, eds. *The Sayings Gospel Q in Greek and English with Parallels from the Gospels of Mark and Thomas*. Edited by Milton Moreland. Contributions to Biblical Exegesis and Theology 30. Leuven: Peeters; Minneapolis: Fortress Press, 2002.

Studies

Cadbury, Henry J. *The Style and Literary Method of Luke*. Harvard Theological Studies 6. Cambridge, MA: Harvard University Press, 1920.

Derrenbacker, Robert A. *Ancient Compositional Practices and the Synoptic Problem*. Bibliotheca Ephemeridum Theologicarum Lovaniensium 186. Leuven: Peeters, 2005.

Dunn, James D. G. *Jesus Remembered*. Vol. 1 of *Christianity in the Making*. Grand Rapids and Cambridge: Wm. B. Eerdmans, 2003.

———. *Unity and Diversity in the New Testament: An Inquiry into the Character of Earliest Christianity*. Philadelphia: Westminster Press, 1977.

Elliott, J. K. *The Language and Style of the Gospel of Mark: An Edition of C. H. Turner's "Marcan Usage" Together with Other Comparable Studies*. Novum Testamentum Supplements 71. Leiden: E. J. Brill, 1993.

Eve, Eric. "Reconstructing Mark: A Thought Experiment." In *Questioning Q: A Multidimensional Critique*, edited by Mark Goodacre and Nicholas Perrin, 89–114. Downers Grove, IL: InterVarsity Press, 2005.

Farmer, William R. *The Synoptic Problem: A Critical Analysis.* New York: Macmillan & Co., 1964.

Goodacre, Mark S. *The Case against Q: Studies in Markan Priority and the Synoptic Problem.* Harrisburg, PA: Trinity Press International, 2002.

Goodman, Martin. "The First Jewish Revolt: Social Conflict and the Problem of Debt." *Journal of Jewish Studies* 33 (1982): 417–27.

Griesbach, Johann Jakob. "A Demonstration That Mark Was Written after Matthew and Luke." In *J. J. Griesbach, Synoptic and Text Critical Studies, 1776–1976,* edited by Bernard Orchard and Thomas R. W. Longstaff. Society for New Testament Studies Monograph Series 34, 103–35. Cambridge and New York: Cambridge University Press, 1978.

Hartin, Patrick J. *James and the "Q" Sayings of Jesus.* Journal for the Study of the New Testament, Supplements 47. Sheffield: Sheffield Academic Press, 1991.

Hezser, Catherine. *Jewish Literacy in Roman Palestine.* Texte und Studien zum Antiken Judentum 81. Tübingen: J. C. B. Mohr (Paul Siebeck), 2001.

Jacobson, Arland D. "The Literary Unity of Q." *Journal of Biblical Literature* 101, no. 3 (1982): 365–89.

Jeremias, Joachim. *Die Sprache des Lukasevangeliums: Redaktion und Tradition im Nicht-Markusstoff des dritten Evangeliums.* Göttingen: Vandenhoeck & Ruprecht, 1980.

Johnson-DeBaufre, Melanie. *Jesus among Her Children: Q, Eschatology, and the Construction of Christian Origins.* Harvard Theological Studies 55. Cambridge, MA: Harvard University Press, 2006.

Kennedy, George A. *Progymnasmata: Greek Textbooks of Prose Composition and Rhetoric.* Atlanta: Society of Biblical Literature, 2003.

Kilpatrick, G. D. "The Disappearance of Q." *Journal of Theological Studies* 42 (1941): 182–84.

Kloppenborg, John S. *Excavating Q: The History and Setting of the Sayings Gospel.* Minneapolis: Fortress Press; Edinburgh: T. & T. Clark, 2000.

———. *The Formation of Q: Trajectories in Ancient Wisdom Collections.* 2000. Studies in Antiquity and Christianity. Philadelphia: Fortress Press, 1987.

———. *The Tenants in the Vineyard: Ideology, Economics, and Agrarian Conflict in Jewish Palestine.* Wissenschaftliche Untersuchungen zum Neuen Testament 195. Tübingen: J. C. B. Mohr [Paul Siebeck], 2006.

———. "City and Wasteland: Narrative World and the Beginning of the Sayings Gospel (Q)." In *How Gospels Begin,* edited by Dennis E. Smith. *Semeia* 52, 145–60. Atlanta: Scholars Press, 1990.

———. "Economic Assumptions of Jesus' Parables." In *Engaging Economics: New Testament Scenarios and Early Christian Interpretation,* edited by Bruce Longenecker and Kelly Liebengood. Grand Rapids: Wm. B. Eerdmans, 2009.

———. "Emulation of the Jesus Tradition in James." In *Reading James with New Eyes,* edited by Robert L. Webb and John S. Kloppenborg. Library of New

Testament Studies 342, 121–50. London and New York: T. & T. Clark International, 2007.

———. "The Growth and Impact of Agricultural Tenancy in Jewish Palestine (III BCE–I CE)." *Journal for the Economic and Social History of the Orient* 51, no. 1 (2008): 33–36.

———. "On Dispensing with Q? Goodacre on the Relation of Luke to Matthew." *New Testament Studies* 49, no. 2 (2003): 210–36.

Koester, Helmut. "GNOMAI DIAPHOROI: The Origin and Nature of Diversification in the History of Early Christianity." In *Trajectories through Early Christianity*, by James M. Robinson and Helmut Koester, 114–57. Philadelphia: Fortress Press, 1971.

———. "Q and Its Relatives." In *Gospel Origins and Christian Beginnings: In Honor of James M. Robinson*, edited by James E. Goehring, Jack T. Sanders, and Charles W. Hedrick, in collaboration with Hans Dieter Betz, 49–63. Sonoma, CA: Polebridge Press, 1990.

———. "The Synoptic Sayings Gospel Q in the Early Communities of Jesus' Followers." In *From Jesus to the Gospels: Interpreting the New Testament in Its Context*, 72–83. Minneapolis: Fortress Press, 2007.

Lührmann, Dieter. "Q: Sayings of Jesus or Logia?" In *The Gospel behind the Gospels: Current Studies on Q*, edited by Ronald A. Piper. Novum Testamentum Supplements 75, 97–116. Leiden, New York, and Köln: E. J. Brill, 1995.

Manson, T. W. *The Sayings of Jesus*. London: SCM Press, 1949.

Neirynck, Frans. *The Minor Agreements of Matthew and Luke against Mark: With a Cumulative List*. Bibliotheca Ephemeridum Theologicarum Lovaniensium 37. Leuven: Leuven University Press, 1974.

Oakman, Douglas E. *Jesus and the Peasants*. Matrix: The Bible in Mediterranean Context. Eugene, OR: Cascade Books, 2008.

———. "Culture, Society, and Embedded Religion in Antiquity." *Biblical Theology Bulletin* 35, no. 1 (2005): 4–12.

Peabody, David L., Lamar Cope, and Allan J. McNicol. *One Gospel from Two: Mark's Use of Matthew and Luke*. Harrisburg, PA: Trinity Press International, 2002.

Piper, Ronald A. "Matthew 7:7–11 par. Luke 11:9–13: Evidence of Design and Argument in the Collection of Jesus' Sayings." In *The Shape of Q: Signal Essays on the Sayings Gospel*, edited by John S. Kloppenborg, 131–37. Minneapolis: Fortress Press, 1994.

Pryke, E. J. *Redactional Style in the Marcan Gospel: A Study of Syntax and Vocabulary as Guides to Redaction in Mark*. Society for New Testament Studies Monograph Series 33. Cambridge and New York: Cambridge University Press, 1978.

Redfield, Robert. *Peasant Society and Culture: An Anthropological Approach to Civilization*. 1989. Chicago: University of Chicago Press, 1965.

Robinson, James M. *The Sayings Gospel Q: Collected Essays*. Edited by Christoph Heil and Joseph Verheyden. Bibliotheca Ephemeridum Theologicarum Lovaniensium 189. Leuven: Peeters, 2005.

————. "LOGOI SOPHON: On the Gattung of Q." In *Trajectories through Early Christianity*, by James M. Robinson and Helmut Koester, 71–113. Philadelphia: Fortress Press, 1971.

Robinson, James M., John S. Kloppenborg, and Paul Hoffmann, gen. eds. *Documenta Q: Reconstructions of Q through Two Centuries of Gospel Research*. Edited by Stanley D. Anderson et al. Leuven: Peeters, 1996–.

Schenk, Wolfgang. *Die Sprache des Matthäus*. Göttingen: Vandenhoeck & Ruprecht, 1987.

Scott, James C. "Protest and Profanation: Agrarian Revolt and the Little Tradition." *Theory and Society* 4 (1977): 1–38, 211–46.

Smith, Daniel A. *The Post-Mortem Vindication of Jesus in the Sayings Gospel Q*. Library of New Testament Studies 338. London and New York: T. & T. Clark International, 2007.

————. "Revisiting the Empty Tomb: The Post-Mortem Vindication of Jesus in Mark and Q." *Novum Testamentum* 45, no. 2 (2003): 123–37.

Streeter, B. H. "The Literary Evolution of the Gospels." In *Oxford Studies in the Synoptic Problem*, edited by William Sanday, 209–27. Oxford: Clarendon Press, 1911.

Wachob, Wesley Hiram. *The Voice of Jesus in the Social Rhetoric of James*. Society for New Testament Studies Monograph Series 106. Cambridge and New York: Cambridge University Press, 2000.

Notes

Introduction

1. *The Critical Edition of Q: A Synopsis, Including the Gospels of Matthew and Luke, Mark and Thomas, with English, German and French Translations of Q and Thomas*, Hermeneia Supplements (Leuven: Peeters; Minneapolis: Fortress Press, 2000); *El Documento Q en griego y en español con paralelos del evangelio de Marcos y del evangelio de Tomás*, ed. Santiago Guijarro, Biblioteca de Estudios Bíblicos 107 (Salamanca: Ediciones Sígueme; Leuven: Peeters, 2002); *Die Logienquelle Q. Der griechische Text in der Rekonstruktion des Internationalen Q-Projekts mit deutscher Übersetzung*, ed. Christoph Heil (Darmstadt: Wissenschaftliche Buchgesellschaft, 2002); *The Sayings Gospel Q in Greek and English with Parallels from the Gospels of Mark and Thomas*, ed. Milton Moreland, Contributions to Biblical Exegesis and Theology 30 (Leuven: Peeters; Minneapolis: Fortress Press, 2002).
2. James M. Robinson, John S. Kloppenborg, and Paul Hoffmann, gen. eds., *Documenta Q: Reconstructions of Q through Two Centuries of Gospel Research*, ed. Stanley D. Anderson et al. (Leuven: Peeters, 1996–). Eight volumes have been published to date.
3. See Dale C. Allison, *The Jesus Tradition in Q* (Valley Forge, PA: Trinity Press International, 1997); Richard A. Horsley and Jonathan A. Draper, *Whoever Hears You Hears Me: Prophets, Performance, and Tradition in Q* (Harrisburg, PA: Trinity Press International, 1999); Arland D. Jacobson, *The First Gospel: An Introduction to Q*, Foundations and Facets: Reference Series (Sonoma, CA: Polebridge Press, 1992); John S. Kloppenborg, *Excavating Q: The History and Setting of the Sayings Gospel* (Minneapolis: Fortress Press; Edinburgh: T. & T. Clark, 2000); Christopher M. Tuckett, *Q and the History of Early Christianity: Studies on Q* (Edinburgh: T. & T. Clark; Peabody, MA: Hendrickson Publishers, 1996).

Chapter One: What Is Q?

1. Kurt Aland, *Synopsis of the Four Gospels: Completely Revised on the Basis of the Greek Text of the Nestle-Aland 26th Edition* (New York: United Bible Societies, 1982); Burton H. Throckmorton, *Gospel Parallels: A Comparison of the*

Synoptic Gospels, 5th ed., revised and updated (Nashville: Thomas Nelson, 1992).

2. See Robert A. Derrenbacker, *Ancient Compositional Practices and the Synoptic Problem*, BETL 186 (Leuven: Peeters, 2005).

3. Johann Jakob Griesbach, "A Demonstration That Mark Was Written after Matthew and Luke," in *J. J. Griesbach, Synoptic and Text Critical Studies, 1776–1976*, ed. Bernard Orchard and Thomas R. W. Longstaff, SNTSMS 34 (Cambridge and New York: Cambridge University Press, 1978), 103.

4. Robert Morgenthaler, *Statistische Synopse* (Zürich and Stuttgart: Gotthelf, 1971), 261, lists the four lowest agreement pericopae as Luke 12:51–53 || Matt. 10:34–35 (11%); Luke 14:35a || Matt. 5:13 (9%); Luke 17:4 || Matt. 18:22b (6%); and Luke 14:5b || Matt. 12:11b (0%). The latter, however, is often not thought to come from Q at all.

5. There are in fact other logically possible solutions that do not involve a direct relationship between Matthew and Luke, but these involve levels of complexity and require incredible assumptions that would render such solutions much less preferable than a simple branch solution. See my discussion in John S. Kloppenborg, *Excavating Q: The History and Setting of the Sayings Gospel* (Minneapolis: Fortress Press; Edinburgh: T. & T. Clark, 2000), 31–32.

6. There is a set of data called the "minor agreements" of Matthew and Luke against Mark. The majority of these have to do with stylistic preferences shared by Matthew and Luke (e.g., substituting more elegant constructions for Mark's excessive use of "and" in joining clauses). Naturally, Matthew and Luke sometimes eliminate Markan parataxis in the same way, but since they do not do so consistently, these agreements should be regarded as coincidental. For a full discussion, see Frans Neirynck, *The Minor Agreements of Matthew and Luke against Mark: With a Cumulative List*, BETL 37 (Leuven: Leuven University Press, 1974).

7. Henry Owen, *Observations on the Four Gospels: Tending Chiefly to Ascertain the Times of Their Publication, and to Illustrate the Form and Manner of Their Composition* (London: T. Payne, 1764).

8. Johan Jakob Griebach, *Commentatio qua Marci Evangelium totum e Matthaei et Lucae commentariis deceŕptum esse monstratur* (Jena: J. C. G. Goepferdt), ET, "Demonstration."

9. Ibid., 107.

10. Ibid., 106.

11. William R. Farmer, *The Synoptic Problem: A Critical Analysis* (New York: Macmillan & Co., 1964), 236–38.

12. David L. Peabody, Lamar Cope, and Allan J. McNicol, *One Gospel from Two: Mark's Use of Matthew and Luke* (Harrisburg, PA: Trinity Press International, 2002), 85.

13. E.g., according to the 2GH, Mark (8:27–20) took over Luke 9:18–21 and ignored the more elaborate version in the parallel Matthean account (16:13–20).
14. Mark S. Goodacre, *The Case against Q: Studies in Markan Priority and the Synoptic Problem* (Harrisburg, PA: Trinity Press International, 2002), 30–31.
15. Advocates of the 2GH do not supply a helpful explanation. Peabody, Cope, and McNicol, *One Gospel from Two*, 107, state: "Luke skipped over a number of sayings in Mt 7:6–15 and came to Mt 7:16–21 where he combined the saying about a tree known by its fruits with a similar saying in Mt 12:33–35. This brought him to the conclusion of the Sermon in Mt 7:21, 24–27 || Luke 6:46–49. . . . Luke made 'hearing and doing' a major feature of his conclusion." This only *describes* what Luke has done; it does not *explain* it.
16. Goodacre, *Case against Q*, 89. It should be observed that this is pure speculation. There is no direct evidence to suggest that Luke came to know Mark before he knew Matthew. This supposition functions purely to let Goodacre escape the dilemma of having Luke know Matthew but nonetheless never be influenced by Matthew's use of Mark.
17. For a full critique of Goodacre's theory, see John S. Kloppenborg, "On Dispensing with Q? Goodacre on the Relation of Luke to Matthew," *New Testament Studies* 49, no. 2 (2003): 210–36, and Derrenbacker, *Ancient Compositional Practices*.

Chapter Two: Reconstructing a Lost Gospel

1. John S. Kloppenborg, *Q Parallels: Synopsis, Critical Notes, & Concordance*, Foundations and Facets: New Testament (Sonoma, CA: Polebridge Press, 1988).
2. Arland Jacobson, "The Literary Unity of Q," *Journal of Biblical Literature* 101, no. 3 (1982): 365–89. This essay is reprinted as "The Literary Unity of Q," in *The Shape of Q: Signal Essays on the Sayings Gospel*, ed. John S. Kloppenborg (Minneapolis: Fortress Press, 1994), 98–115.
3. Eric Eve, "Reconstructing Mark: A Thought Experiment," in *Questioning Q: A Multidimensional Critique*, ed. Mark Goodacre and Nicholas Perrin (Downers Grove, IL: InterVarsity Press, 2005), 89–114.
4. Matthew and Luke both omit Mark 1:1; 2:27; 3:20–21; 4:26–29; 7:3–4; 7:32–37; 8:22–26; 9:29; 9:48–49; 13:33–37; 14:51–52.
5. Charles E. Carlston and Dennis Norlin, "Once More—Statistics and Q," *Harvard Theological Review* 64 (1971): 59–78; "Statistics and Q—Some Further Observations," *Novum Testamentum* 41, no. 2 (1999): 108–23.
6. See John S. Kloppenborg, *Excavating Q: The History and Setting of the Sayings Gospel* (Minneapolis: Fortress Press; Edinburgh: T. & T. Clark, 2000), 95–96.
7. James M. Robinson, Paul Hoffmann, and John S. Kloppenborg, eds., *The Critical Edition of Q: A Synopsis, Including the Gospels of Matthew and Luke,*

Mark and Thomas, with English, German and French Translations of Q and Thomas, Hermeneia Supplements (Leuven: Peeters; Minneapolis: Fortress Press, 2000).

8. Kloppenborg, *Q Parallels.*

9. In contrast to Mark, Matthew and Luke have (a) a participial form of "baptize"; (b) "open" instead of "tear" ; (c) describe the Spirit descending "upon (*epi*) him" rather than "to (*eis*) him"; and (d) both place "descend" before "as a dove."

10. The International Q Project reflects the same division. Initial discussions concluded that it should be excluded, but two of the three editors of the Critical Edition argued for its inclusion (Robinson, Hoffmann, and Kloppenborg, *Critical Edition of Q,* 18). Kloppenborg was the dissenting opinion.

11. John S. Kloppenborg, "City and Wasteland: Narrative World and the Beginning of the Sayings Gospel (Q)," in *How Gospels Begin,* ed. Dennis E. Smith, *Semeia* 52 (Atlanta: Scholars Press, 1990), 151–52.

12. See Kloppenborg, *Q Parallels,* 209. On the basis of my 1988 tabulation, Matthew and Luke agree on 2,414 of Matthew's 4,464 "Q" words, or 54.08%, and on 2,414 of Luke's 4,652 "Q" words, or 51.59%.

13. For Markan style, see E. J. Pryke, *Redactional Style in the Marcan Gospel: A Study of Syntax and Vocabulary as Guides to Redaction in Mark,* SNTSMS 33 (Cambridge and New York: Cambridge University Press, 1978), and J. K. Elliott, *The Language and Style of the Gospel of Mark: An Edition of C. H. Turner's "Marcan Usage" Together with Other Comparable Studies,* NovTSup 71 (Leiden: E. J. Brill, 1993). For Matthew, see Wolfgang Schenk, *Die Sprache des Matthäus* (Göttingen: Vandenhoeck & Ruprecht, 1987); for Luke, see Henry J. Cadbury, *The Style and Literary Method of Luke,* reprint, Kraus Reprint Co. 1969, HTS 6 (Cambridge, MA: Harvard University Press, 1920), and Joachim Jeremias, *Die Sprache des Lukasevangeliums: Redaktion und Tradition im Nicht-Markusstoff des dritten Evangeliums* (Göttingen: Vandenhoeck & Ruprecht, 1980).

14. The major publication is Robinson, Hoffmann, and Kloppenborg, *Critical Edition of Q* (2000). A briefer version, containing the Greek and English texts of Q and a concordance, is available as James M. Robinson, Paul Hoffmann, and John S. Kloppenborg, eds., *The Sayings Gospel Q in Greek and English with Parallels from the Gospels of Mark and Thomas,* ed. Milton Moreland, Contributions to Biblical Exegesis and Theology 30 (Leuven: Peeters; Minneapolis: Fortress Press, 2002). The dababase is published as James M. Robinson, John S. Kloppenborg, and Paul Hoffmann, gen. eds., *Documenta Q: Reconstructions of Q through Two Centuries of Gospel Research,* ed. Stanley D. Anderson et al. (Leuven: Uitgeverij Peeters, 1996–). The first of more than thirty volumes appeared in 1996; eight have subsequently been published.

15. William V. Harris, *Ancient Literacy* (Cambridge, MA: Harvard University Press, 1989); Catherine Hezser, *Jewish Literacy in Roman Palestine,* Texte

und Studien Zum Antiken Judentum 81 (Tübingen: J. C. B. Mohr [Paul Siebeck], 2001), estimates a 3% literacy rate in Jewish Palestine. We should distinguish various levels of literacy: complete illiteracy; signature literacy (the ability to write or read one's signature); craft literacy (the ability to read simple instructions relating to one's craft); administrative literacy (the ability to compose documents with standard forms and formulae such as lists, accounts, leases, wills, marriage agreements); and full literacy—the ability to compose and read complex literary texts. Full literacy was likely found only in the highest levels of society and probably represented only 1% of the population. See Douglas E. Oakman, *Jesus and the Peasants*, Matrix: The Bible in Mediterranean Context (Eugene, OR: Cascade Books, 2008), 298–300.

16. Kloppenborg, *Excavating Q*, 63.

17. James D. G. Dunn, *Jesus Remembered* 1 of *Christianity in the Making* (Grand Rapids, and Cambridge: Wm. B. Eerdmans, 2003); Terence C. Mournet, *Oral Tradition and Literary Dependency: Variability and Stability in the Synoptic Tradition and Q*, WUNT 2/85 (Tübingen: J. C. B. Mohr [Paul Siebeck], 2005).

18. Robert A. Derrenbacker, *Ancient Compositional Practices and the Synoptic Problem*, BETL 186 (Leuven: Peeters, 2005); John S. Kloppenborg, "Variation in the Reproduction of the Double Tradition and an Oral Q?" *Ephemerides theologicae lovanienses* 83, no. 1 (2007): 49–79.

19. See John S. Kloppenborg, *The Formation of Q: Trajectories in Ancient Wisdom Collections*, Studies in Antiquity and Christianity (Philadelphia: Fortress Press, 1987), chap. 2.

20. Jonathan L. Reed, *Archaeology and the Galilean Jesus: A Re-Examination of the Evidence* (Harrisburg, PA: Trinity Press International, 2000); Kloppenborg, *Excavating Q*, 171–75; Helmut Koester, "The Synoptic Sayings Gospel Q in the Early Communities of Jesus' Followers," in *From Jesus to the Gospels: Interpreting the New Testament in Its Context* (Minneapolis: Fortress Press, 2007), 72–83.

21. See John S. Kloppenborg, "The Formation of Q and Antique Instructional Genres," *Journal of Biblical Literature* 105, no. 3 (1986): 443–62, and *Formation*, chap. 7.

22. Alan Kirk, "Administrative Writing, Oral Tradition, and Q," paper read at the Annual Meeting of the Society of Biblical Literature, Q Section (2004). For example *P.Amherst* 33 (ca. 157 BCE): "To King Ptolemy and Queen Kleopatra the sister, Mother-loving Gods, greetings from Marepathis son of Sisouchos . . . [followed by the names of four other co-petitioners], royal farmers of Soknopaiou Nasos in the division of Herakleides in the Arsinoite nome. . . . [Then follows a description of a legal case where the petitioners fear that their opponent will come with a lawyer, contrary to the law governing courts for setting native cases]. We ask you, the greatest gods, if it please you, to send our petition to the *chresmatistae* [judges] in order that

when the examination of petitions is held, they may forbid Tesenouphis to appear in court with a lawyer. For this measure will prevent your interests from suffering harm. Farewell" (from A. S. Hunt and C. C. Edgar, *Select Papyri*, LCL [London: William Heinemann; Cambridge, MA: Harvard University Press, 1932–34], 2:245–49 [no. 273]).

23. Kirk, "Administrative Writing," 8.

24. Friedrich F. Hiller von Gaertringen, ed., *Inschriften von Priene*, ed. Carl Johann Fredrich (Berlin: Georg Reimer; Walter de Gruyter, 1906), no. 105.

Chapter Three: What a Difference Difference Makes

1. This does not necessarily imply that the Q people would agree with the application of the Pharisees' theory of taxation. See John S. Kloppenborg, *Excavating Q: The History and Setting of the Sayings Gospel* (Minneapolis: Fortress Press; Edinburgh: T. & T. Clark, 2000), 225–27, 258–59.

2. Pss. 65:7; 89:9; 93:4; 107:25, 29; 148:8.

3. T. W. Manson, *The Sayings of Jesus* (London: SCM Press, 1949), 9.

4. B. H. Streeter, "The Literary Evolution of the Gospels," in *Oxford Studies in the Synoptic Problem*, ed. William Sanday (Oxford: Clarendon Press, 1911), 212–19.

5. Benjamin Wiser Bacon, "The Nature and Design of Q, the Second Synoptic Source," *Hibbert Journal* 22 (1923–24): 688 (emphasis original).

6. See the helpful treatment in Arland J. Hultgren, *The Rise of Normative Christianity* (Minneapolis: Fortress Press, 1994), 31–41.

7. Mark 8:34: "If someone wants to follow me, let him deny himself and pick up [*aratō*] his cross and follow me."

8. The basic study of the Deuteronomistic view of history and of prophecy is Odil H. Steck, *Israel und das gewaltsame Geschick der Propheten: Untersuchungen zur Überlieferung des deuteronomistischen Geschichtsbildes im Alten Testament, Spätjudentum und Urchristentum*, WMANT 23 (Neukirchen-Vluyn: Neukirchener Verlag, 1967). In the Hebrew Bible, see Deut. 4:25–31; 28:45–68 + 30:1–10; 1 Kgs. 8:46–53; Jer. 7:25–34; 25:4–14; 29:17–20; 35:15–17; 44:2–14; Lam. 3:42–47; Dan. 9:4b–19; Zech. 1:2–6; 7:4–14; 2 Chr. 15:1–7; 29:5–11; 30:6–9; Ezra 9:6–15; Neh. 1:5–11; 9:5–37. In the literature of Second Temple Judaism: Bar. 1:15–3:8; 3:9–4:4; 4:5–5:9; Tob. 3:1–6; 13:3–6; *Testament of Levi* 10.2–5; 14; 15.1–4; 16.1–5; *Testament of Judah* 23.1–5; *Testament of Issachar* 6.1–4; *Testament of Zebulum* 9.5–9; *Testament of Dan* 5.4–9; *Testament of Naphthali* 4.1–5; *Testament of Asher* 7.2–7; *1 Enoch* 93.1–10 + 91.12–17; 85–90; 91–104; *Jubilees* 1.7–26; the *Damascus Covenant* 20.28–30; 1.3–13a; 4QDibHam 1.8–7.2; *Psalms of Solomon* 2:9; 8:2; 17:17; *4 Ezra* 3.4–25, 27; 7.129–30; 14.27–35; Pseudo Philo, *Biblical Antiquites* 2; *2 Apocalypse of Baruch* 1:1–5; 4:1–6; 31:1–32:7; 44:1–46:7; 77:1–17; 78–87.

9. See John S. Kloppenborg, "*Exitus Clari Viri*: The Death of Jesus in Luke," *Toronto Journal of Theology* 8, no. 1 (1992): 106–20; Gregory E. Sterling,

"Mors Philosophi: The Death of Jesus in Luke," *Harvard Theological Review* 94, no. 4 (2001): 383–402.

10. Isa. 26:19; 29:18–19, 35:5–6, 42:7, and 61:1.

11. Daniel A. Smith, "Revisiting the Empty Tomb: The Post-Mortem Vindication of Jesus in Mark and Q," *Novum Testamentum* 45, no. 2 (2003): 123–37; *The Post-Mortem Vindication of Jesus in the Sayings Gospel Q*, LNTS 338 (London and New York: T. & T. Clark International, 2007), and earlier, Dieter Zeller, "Entrückung zur Ankunft als Menschensohn (Lk 13,34f.; 11:29f.)," in *A cause de l'évangile: études sur les Synoptiques et les Actes: offertes au P. Jacques Dupont, O.S.B. à l'occasion de son 70ᵉ anniversaire*, Lectio Divina 123 (Paris: Publications de Saint-André; Les Editions du Cerf, 1985), 513–30.

12. Gerhard Lohfink, *Die Himmelfahrt Jesu: Untersuchungen zu den Himmelfahrts- und Erhöhungstexten bei Lukas*, SANT 26 (München: Kösel Verlag, 1971), 41–42. A second set of terms associated with assumption is *harpazein*, "to snatch away," and *methistēmi*, "to remove." Paul uses *harpazein* of the catching up of the faithful in 1 Thess. 4:13–18, and which also appears in several Greek stories of the "snatching up" of a hero to save the hero from an ignominious death.

13. See *2 Bar.* 13.3; 25.1; 76.2; *4 Ezra* 14.9; 50 [Syriac]. Of the righteous in general: *4 Ezra* 6.26; 7.38; 13.52.

14. Zeller, "Entrückung," 518.

15. See Smith, "Revisiting the Empty Tomb."

16. See Martin Goodman, "The First Jewish Revolt: Social Conflict and the Problem of Debt," *Journal of Jewish Studies* 33 (1982): 417–27.

17. Douglas E. Oakman, "Culture, Society, and Embedded Religion in Antiquity," *Biblical Theology Bulletin* 35, no. 1 (2005): 6.

18. Robert Redfield, *Peasant Society and Culture: An Anthropological Approach to Civilization* (Chicago: University of Chicago Press, 1965), 41–44, here 41–42: "In a civilization there is a great tradition of the reflective few, and there is a little tradition of the largely unreflective many. The great tradition is cultivated in schools or temples; the little tradition works itself out and keeps going in the lives of the unlettered in their village communities. The tradition of the philosopher, theologian, and literary man is a tradition consciously cultivated and handed down; that of the little people is for the most part taken for granted and not submitted to much scrutiny or considered refinement and improvement."

19. James C. Scott, "Protest and Profanation: Agrarian Revolt and the Little Tradition," *Theory and Society* 4 (1977): 13. Scott's example is South Asia: "Thus we find lower class Hindus Sanskritizing their culture to improve their ritual status while contemporary Brahmins are busily becoming westernized." An analogous situation may have developed in Jewish Palestine, between the nonelite, influenced both by the great traditions of the Pentateuch and prophets and by the ideology of the Maccabees, and the elite

who had already been subject to Hellenization and Romanization in significant respects.

20. Josephus, *War* 2.427. See Goodman, "The Problem of Debt."

21. Scott, "Protest and Profanations," 4.

22. Arthur Stinchcombe, "Agricultural Enterprise and Rural Class Relations," *American Journal of Sociology* 67 (1961–62): 186.

23. See John S. Kloppenborg, "The Growth and Impact of Agricultural Tenancy in Jewish Palestine (III BCE–I CE)," *Journal for the Economic and Social History of the Orient* 51, no. 1 (2008): 33–66; Paul Erdkamp, "Agriculture, Underemployment, and the Cost of Rural Labour in the Roman World," *Classical Quarterly* 49, no. 2 (1999): 556–72.

24. See John S. Kloppenborg, "Economic Assumptions of Jesus' Parables," in *Engaging Economics: New Testament Scenarios and Early Christian Interpretation*, ed. Bruce Longenecker and Kelly Liebengood (Grand Rapids: Wm. B. Eerdmans, 2009), forthcoming.

25. Douglas E. Oakman, *Jesus and the Peasants*, Matrix: The Bible in Mediterranean Context (Eugene, OR: Cascade Books, 2008), 236.

26. Ibid., 289.

27. Ibid., 290.

28. Melanie Johnson-DeBaufre, *Jesus among Her Children: Q, Eschatology, and the Construction of Christian Origins*, HTS 55 (Cambridge, MA: Harvard University Press, 2006), 167. This is a welcome corrective to the view that I took in *The Formation of Q: Trajectories in Ancient Wisdom Collections*, Studies in Antiquity and Christianity (Philadelphia: Fortress Press, 1987), 124–25.

29. Johnson-DeBaufre, *Jesus among Her Children*, 61.

30. Gerhard Kittel and Gerhard Friedrich, eds., *Theological Dictionary of the New Testament*, trans. Geoffrey W. Bromiley (Grand Rapids: Wm. B. Eerdmans, 1963–75), 4:365.

31. Burton L. Mack, "Lord of the Logia: Savior or Sage?" in *Gospel Origins and Christian Beginnings: In Honor of James M. Robinson*, ed. James E. Goehring et al. (Sonoma, CA: Polebridge Press, 1990), 18.

32. John Dominic Crossan, "Itinerants and Householders in the Earliest Kingdom Movement," in *Reimagining Christian Origins: A Colloquium Honoring Burton L. Mack*, ed. Elizabeth Castelli and Hal Taussig (Valley Forge, PA: Trinity Press International, 1996), 117.

Chapter Four: Q, *Thomas*, and James

1. G. D. Kilpatrick, "The Disappearance of Q," *Journal of Theological Studies* 42 (1941): 182–84.

2. James D. G. Dunn, *Unity and Diversity in the New Testament: An Inquiry into the Character of Earliest Christianity* (Philadelphia: Westminster Press, 1977), 287.

3. James M. Robinson, "LOGOI SOPHON: On the Gattung of Q," in *Trajectories through Early Christianity*, by James M. Robinson and Helmut Koester (Philadelphia: Fortress Press, 1971), 71–113.

4. John S. Kloppenborg, *The Formation of Q: Trajectories in Ancient Wisdom Collections*, Studies in Antiquity and Christianity (Philadelphia: Fortress Press, 1987), chap. 7.

5. James M. Robinson, "On Bridging the Gulf from Q to the Gospel of Thomas (or Vice Versa)," in *Nag Hammadi and Early Christianity*, ed. Charles W. Hedrick and Robert Hodgson (Peabody, MA: Hendrickson, 1986), 136–37.

6. Dieter Lührmann, "Q: Sayings of Jesus or Logia?" in *The Gospel behind the Gospels: Current Studies on Q*, ed. Ronald A. Piper, NovTSup 75 (Leiden, New York, and Köln: E. J. Brill, 1995), 113.

7. Andrew Gregory, *The Reception of Luke and Acts in the Period before Irenaeus*, WUNT 2/169 (Tübingen: J. C. B. Mohr [Paul Siebeck], 2003), 128.

8. See John S. Kloppenborg, "The Growth and Impact of Agricultural Tenancy in Jewish Palestine (III BCE–I CE)," *Journal for the Economic and Social History of the Orient* 51, no. 1 (2008): 33–66.

9. See John S. Kloppenborg, "The Use of the Synoptics or Q in Did. 1.3b–2.1," in *The Didache and Matthew: Two Documents from the Same Jewish-Christian Milieu?* ed. Huub van de Sandt (Assen: Van Gorcum; Minneapolis: Fortress Press, 2005), 105–29.

10. B. P. Grenfell and A. S. Hunt, *ΛΟΓΙΑ ΙΗΣΟΥ: The Sayings of Our Lord from an Early Greek Papyrus* (London: Henry Frowde, for the Egypt Exploration Fund, 1897), 18. Similarly, Benjamin Wiser Bacon, "Logia," in *A Dictionary of Christ and the Gospels*, ed. James Hastings (New York: Charles Scribner's Sons; Edinburgh: T. & T. Clark, 1908), 45: "The discovery of Grenfell and Hunt of papyri of the 2nd and 3rd century, in which sayings attributed to Jesus are agglutinated with no more of narrative framework than the bare words 'Jesus saith' (*legei Iesous*), proves that such compilations actually circulated, fulfilling a function similar to the *Pirke Aboth*, or the 'Sayings of the Fathers' in the contemporary and earlier Synagogue."

11. Robinson, "LOGOI SOPHON"; Helmut Koester, "GNOMAI DIAPHOROI: The Origin and Nature of Diversification in the History of Early Christianity," in *Trajectories through Early Christianity*, by James M. Robinson and Helmut Koester (Philadelphia: Fortress Press, 1971), 114–57. Neither Robinson nor Koester referred to Q as a "gospel" in 1971, but both subsequently have embraced this nomenclature: James M. Robinson, *The Sayings Gospel Q: Collected Essays*, ed. Christoph Heil and Joseph Verheyden, BETL 189 (Leuven: Peeters, 2005); Helmut Koester, "The Synoptic Sayings Gospel Q in the Early Communities of Jesus' Followers," in *From Jesus to the Gospels: Interpreting the New Testament in Its Context* (Minneapolis: Fortress Press, 2007), 72–83.

12. See John S. Kloppenborg, *The Tenants in the Vineyard: Ideology, Economics, and Agrarian Conflict in Jewish Palestine*, WUNT 195 (Tübingen: J. C. B. Mohr [Paul Siebeck], 2006), chap. 8.

13. See Kloppenborg, *Formation*; Max Küchler, *Frühjüdische Weisheitstraditionen: Zum Fortgang weisheitlichen Denkens im Bereich des frühjüdischen Jahweglaubens*, OBO 26 (Göttingen: Vandenhoeck & Ruprecht; Freiburg/Sw: Universitätsverlag, 1979).

14. See John Dominic Crossan, *The Birth of Christianity: Discovering What Happened in the Years Immediately after the Execution of Jesus* (San Francisco: HarperSanFrancisco, 1998), 587–91. Crossan in fact divides Thomas into 132 units, since some of its sayings are composite, and Q into 101 units. According to his calculations, 28% (37/132) of the *Gospel of Thomas* has parallels in Q, and 37% (37/101) of Q has parallels in Thomas (254).

15. I use here the divisions of Q by the International Q Project: James M. Robinson, Paul Hoffmann, and John S. Kloppenborg, eds., *The Sayings Gospel Q in Greek and English with Parallels from the Gospels of Mark and Thomas*, ed. Milton Moreland, Contributions to Biblical Exegesis and Theology 30 (Leuven: Peeters; Minneapolis: Fortress Press, 2002).

16. Helmut Koester, "Q and Its Relatives," in *Gospel Origins and Christian Beginnings: In Honor of James M. Robinson*, ed. James E. Goehring et al. (Sonoma, CA: Polebridge Press, 1990), 60.

17. Patrick J. Hartin, *James and the "Q" Sayings of Jesus*, JSNTSup 47 (Sheffield: Sheffield Academic Press, 1991), chaps. 5–6.

18. The principal exception is James 5:12, the prohibition against taking oaths, attested only in Matt. 5:34–37, but in a form that does not suggest knowledge of Matthew.

19. Hartin, *James and the "Q" Sayings*, 186.

20. For a fuller discussion, see John S. Kloppenborg, "Emulation of the Jesus Tradition in James," in *Reading James with New Eyes*, ed. Robert L. Webb and John S. Kloppenborg, Library of New Testament Studies 342 (London and New York: T. & T. Clark International, 2007), 121–50.

21. In the Hebrew Bible one seeks or finds "wisdom" (Job 28:12–13, 20; 32:13; Prov. 1:28; 2:4; 3:13; 8:17; 14:6; Qoh. 7:25; Sir. 4:11; 6:18; 18:28; 25:10; 51:20, 26; Wis. 6:12), "knowledge of God" (Prov. 2:5; 8:9), "understanding" (Sir. 25:9), "grace" (Prov. 3:3; 12:3), "life" (Prov. 21:21), "rest" (Sir. 28:16), and "instruction" (Sir. 51:13, 16).

22. See Ronald A. Piper, "Matthew 7:7–11 par. Luke 11:9–13: Evidence of Design and Argument in the Collection of Jesus' Sayings," in *The Shape of Q: Signal Essays on the Sayings Gospel*, ed. John S. Kloppenborg (Minneapolis: Fortress Press, 1994), 132.

23. George A. Kennedy, *Progymnasmata: Greek Textbooks of Prose Composition and Rhetoric* (Atlanta: Society of Biblical Literature, 2003), 78.

24. Ibid., 100.

25. See Kloppenborg, "Emulation"; Wesley Hiram Wachob, *The Voice of Jesus in the Social Rhetoric of James*, SNTSMS 106 (Cambridge and New York: Cambridge University Press, 2000).

Appendix: The Sayings Gospel Q in English

1. The majority view of the editors of the *Critical Edition* was to include the baptism of Jesus in Q. I was the minority position on the editorial committee.

2. The *Critical Edition* treats Luke 6:24–26 as if it were a Lukan addition to Q. I have argued, on the contrary, that the woes were present in Q, patterned on the Beatitudes.

3. Because of the almost complete verbal disagreement between Matthew and Luke, the IQP has refrained from reconstructing anything. There are also a few scholars who believe the story ended with 7:9 and that there was no confirmation of the healing. I think this unlikely, and so propose an ending to the story, but with no confidence in respect to its wording.

4. The IQP decided against including Luke 9:61–62 in Q, which implies that Luke himself added the third anecdote. I think that sufficient grounds exist to include this in Q. Since there is no Matthean version, it is impossible to be confident about its wording.

5. The *Critical Edition* did not include the full Matthaean portion of the woe against Capernaum, assuming that it was a Matthaean expansion. I believe there are grounds for including it in Q.

6. The IQP voted to include this in Q, but with the lowest level of probability {D}. I have supplied the wording from Q, enclosed in « ».

7. Q 12:13–14, 16–21 is not included in the *Critical Edition*, but I have argued elsewhere that good reasons can be adduced to believing it to be a part of Q. See John S. Kloppenborg, *Q Parallels: Synopsis, Critical Notes, & Concordance*, Foundations and Facets: New Testament (Sonoma, CA: Polebridge Press, 1988), 128–29.

8. I here disagree with the sequence of Q 12:22b–31 and 33–34 printed in the *Critical Edition* and the judgment of my two colleagues, who argued that Matthew's sequence (Matt. 6:19–21 [Q 12:33–34]), 25–34 [Q 12:22–31b) is more original than Luke's.

9. The IQP included 17:28–29 at a {D} level, which means that no text is printed. I have included the Lukan wording, *exempli gratia*.

Index

1 Clement, 109, 120
1 Corinthians, 75
1QWords of Moses, 90
2GH (Two Gospel Hypothesis), 20, 22–28
4Q521, 81

Abraham, 50
Aphthonius, 117
appearance stories
   on the 2GH, 24–25
Aramaic original of Q, 58
Aramaisms, 58–59
arboriculture, 89
argument from order, 9
argument from the contrary, 117
assumption, 82, 84
Augustus, 60, 85

Bacon, B. W., 73
baptism of Jesus, 65
   in Q, 48–49
Baruch, 83
beatitudes, 42, 110

Matthew's moralizing
   of, 52
   original wording of, 52
   in Q, 54, 95
Beelzebul, 71
Bethsaida, 67–68
black holes, 63–64

Capernaum, 66–68, 70
catchwords, 107–8
centurion, 68, 70
Chester Beatty I papyrus, 38, 100
chria, 66, 115–16
Christology, 95
circuit of the Jordan, 50, 65
circumcision, 69
cities
   in Luke, 68
   in Matthew, 67
Clement of Rome, 101
communal relationships, 96
conflation, 8, 22
countryside
   in Q, 68

Critical Edition of Q, viii, x, 53, 124
    grading system, 53–54
Crossan, John Dominic, 97
crucifixion, 65

day laborers, 89
death of Jesus, viii
    not in Q, 64
death of the prophets, 76
debt 59–60, 88–92, 96–97
    cancellation of, 90
Deuteronomistic theology, 76–78,
    111
    view of the prophets, 76, 78,
    83
Dialogue of the Savior, 113
Didache, 99, 103–6, 109, 120
Diogenes of Sinope, 115
disappearance and reappearance,
    83, 84
discipleship in, Q
    willingness to suffer, 75
divorce, 60
Documenta Q, viii
double entrendre, 93
double-souled, 118–19
Double Tradition, 13
    placement relative to Mark, 16,
    17
    sequence of, 18–19
Dunn, James D. G., 99–100

Elijah, 76, 83
    assumption of, 82
Enoch, 83
    assumption of, 83
Enslin, Morton, 28
entrusted money, parable of, 56–57
epithymiai (desires), 118

euaggelion (Gospel), 60–61, 74
euaggelizesthai, 61
Eusebius, 57
Eve, Eric, 45
examples from history, 117
exorcisms, 69
Ezekiel, 37, 78
Ezra, 83

family of Jesus, 11
Farmer, William R., 23
Farrer-Goulder hypothesis, 20,
    28–31
festivals, 85
flash floods, 89
friendship, 119
    with God, 119

general reciprocity, 91
Gentiles, 68
Goodacre, Mark S., 1, 24, 28–29
Gospel of Judas, viii, 62
Gospel of Peter, 98
Gospel of Philip, viii, 1, 61
Gospel of the Ebionites, 3, 98
Gospel of the Egyptians, 98
Gospel of the Hebrews, 98,
    113
Gospel of the Savior, viii
Gospel of Thomas viii, 1, 61, 62, 65,
    73–74, 79, 106–7, 109, 110,
    111, 113, 120
Gospel of Truth, 61
Goulder, Michael G., 28
Great Supper, parable of, 56–57
great tradition, 87–88
Gregory, Andrew, 102
Griesbach, Johann Jakob, 10, 22
Griesbach hypothesis, 20, 22–28

Hannukah, 85
Harnack, Adolf, viii
Hartin, Patrick J., 112
Hermogenes, 116
Hesiod, 115
Homer, 115–16
housebuilding, 89
hypotheses
    nature of, 39–40

infancy stories, 22
    on the 2GH, 22, 23
instruction, 59
International Q Project, 46, 53
inversionary language, 95
Ioudaios (Judean), x
Isocrates, 115

Jacobson, Arland D., 44
James, 111
    urban setting, 120
    use of Q by, 112, 114
Jerusalem, 67–68
Jesus and John, 94
Jesus' death
    in Luke, 78–79
    in Matthew, 78
    Q's understanding, 73–76,
        78–79
Jesus' postmortem vindication, 84
Jesus' vindication
    as assumption, 83–84
John's question about Jesus,
    70
Johnson-Debaufre, Melanie, 94
Jonah, 71
Jordan rift valley, 67
Josephus, 88
Judeans, x

kashrut, 68–69
kerygma, 73, 107
Khorazin, 67–68
Kilpatrick, G. D., 98
kingdom of God, 120
Kinneret, 66
Kirk, Alan, 60
Kloppenborg, John S., 1
Koester, Helmut, 111
komogrammateus (village scribe), 59

landlords, 89, 96
leases, 59, 89
literacy rates, 55
literary dependence, 2–5
little tradition, 87–88
loans, 89, 90
Logia Iēsou, 106
logoi, 74
Lord's Prayer, 58, 60, 89, 92, 113
    on the 2GH, 24
Lost Drachma, parable of the, 47
Lost Sheep, parable of the, 47
Lot, 49, 50
Lucian of Samosata, 66
Lührmann, Dieter, 100
Luke, Gospel of
    improvements of Mark by, 12

m. 'Abot, 66, 100
Mack, Burton L., 97
mammon, 96, 109, 119
Manson, T. W., 73–74
Mark, Gospel of
    medial position of, 5–9
    priority of, 9–12
    stylistically inferior to Matthew
        and Luke, 11
    use of geography, 66

Mark without Q hypothesis, 28–31
    Luke's prior knowledge of Mark,
        29–30
Markan omissions, 10
Mark-Q overlaps, 17, 31, 34, 43
Matthew
    improvements of Mark by, 12
measure-for-measure, 91, 102
micro-conflation, 9
mimetics, 97
"minimal Q," 44–45, 51
minor agreements, 31, 35–37
    Deutero-Markus and the, 38
    oral interference and the, 38
    scribal interference and
        the, 38
miracles stories, 69, 70
    in John, 72
    in Luke, 72
    in Matthew, 72
    in Q, 70–72
    as a sign of the kingdom, 70–71
mnemonics, 97
Morgenthaler, Robert, 1
Mustard Seed, parable of the
    in Mark, 42
    in Q, 42, 43
MwQH, 20, 28–31

Nazara, 65, 67–68
Nehemiah, 77
Neirynck, Frans, 1
Nineveh, 67–68, 71
noble death, 79
nonappearance, 82
nonslave laborers, 90

Oakman, Douglas E., 86, 92–93
One to Come, 97
oral performance, 60, 120

oral-aural-scribal culture, 55, 120
order in the Synoptics
    nonagreement of Matthew and
        Luke against Mark, 9
Origen, 89
Owen, Henry, 22

Papias, 57, 107
Papyrus Egerton 2, 98
Papyrus Oxyrhynchus 1, 106
Papyrus Oxyrhynchus 654, 74, 106,
    113
Papyrus Oxyrhynchus 655, 106
Papyrus Oxyrhynchus 840, 98
Papyrus Oxyrhynchus 1224, 98
paraphrase, 115–17, 119
parasitoi (parasites), 116
Passover, 85
patrilocal marriage, 14
Peabody, David B., 1, 24
petitions, 59
Pharisees, 69
Philostratus, 66
pilgrimage, 87
Polag, Athansius, viii
postmortem vindication, 82, 84
prayer, 113
progymnasmata (preliminary exer-
    cises), 116, 117
proof texts, 117
prophets
    as repentance preachers, 76
Proverbs, 99
ptochoi (beggars), 95

Q
    and special material, 46–48
    as a "Gospel," 60–61, 73
    as a Judean Gospel, 69
    as a "sayings Gospel," 65

as a written text, 55
disappearance of, 98–101
literary organization, 66–68,
    109
oral or written? 55–57
original extent of, 43–48,
    50–51
original language of, 57–59
original wording of, 51–55
performed orally, 55
preservation by Matthew and
    Luke, 45
rural aspects, 69, 88
use of geography, 66–67
quadran, 92
Queen of the South, 71
Quelle, 2, 15
Quintilian, 116–17

rationale, 117–18
Redfield, Robert, 86
reign of God, 96
    and subsistence, 96
religion
    as discrete aspect of culture, 85
    and the elite, 86
    as embedded, 85–86
    and the nonelite, 86
rents, 89–90
re-oralization, 37
resurrection, viii, 65
    in Paul, 80
    in Q, 80, 81
    in Second Temple Judaism, 82
resurrection of Jesus, 80
    in Mark, 80
rhetorical education, 117
rhetorical schools, 115
ritualized friendship, 119
Robinson, James M., 99–100

Ropes, James, 28

Sabbath, 68–69
Sayings Gospel Q, 61
Schenk, Wolfgang, viii
Scott, James C., 87
search-find aphorism, 113
scribal conventions, 59
scribes, 59
Sentences of Sextus, 100
Sepphoris, 93
Sermon at Nazareth
    on the 2GH, 24
Sermon on the Mount
    on the 2GH, 23–24
Sermon on the Plain, 27
    on the 2GH, 23
Shavuot, 86
shepherding, 89
Sidon, 67–68
Simon of Cyrene, 75
Ṣippôrîm (birds), 93
Sirach, 59
slavery, 119
Smith, Daniel A., 82
Socrates, 79
Sodom, 49, 66–67, 111
Solomon, 71
Son of Man, 97, 111
Sophia, 97, 99
"special material," 46
stilling of the storm, 70
Stoicism, 119
storehouse economies, 93
Streeter, B. H., 73
subsistence, 60, 89, 96
Sukkôt, 86
symbolic topography, 67

tax collection, 59, 92, 93

taxes, 88–89
temptation story, 42, 65
    in Mark, 42
    in Q, 42, 55
tenant farmers, 90
Tertullian, 94
Theognis, 115, 117
"this generation," 95
tithes, 69
translation hypotheses, 58
transmission of the Gospels, 38
Two Document hypothesis (2DH),
    15–20, 21, 31
Two Gospel hypothesis (2GH),
    22–28
    relation of Luke to Matthew,
        25–26

Tyre, 67–68

United Bible Societies, 123, 53
utopia, 96

verbatim agreement, 13–14
    low agreement, 56
    varying degrees of, 56–57

wealth, 110
Wisdom of Solomon, 83
    assumption of the just
        man, 83

Yohanan ben Zakkai, 66

Zeller, Dieter, 83